Art is universal i can say its infinite as many as things exsist in the universe its is art from the artist point of view it can be modified changed according to artist choice, so technicaly artist are blessed with abundance of choice's to create art , cartoon can be done by anything from, sun, moon, earth, stars, atom's, the list will go on and on, simple just add some eyes and funny experssions to them they become cartoon i know its not as easy as iam saying however once you learn tricks and technique itl be easy

FA3

Content

Face
Hair, Eyes, Nose

Mouth, lips, teeth and expressions

Body
Full length body, hands and legs

Postures

Perspective
3 2 1

Using golden ratio basics

FA3

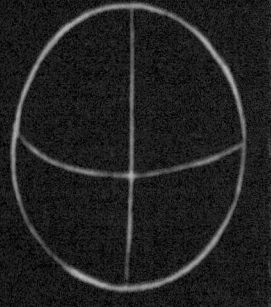 **START WITH BASIC CIRCLE**

LENGTHEN IT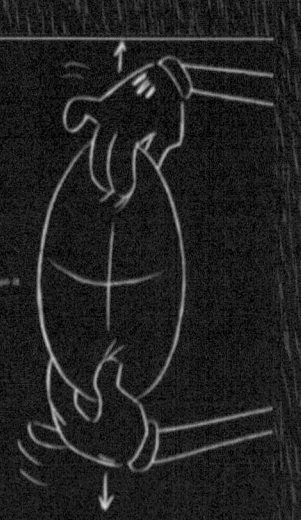

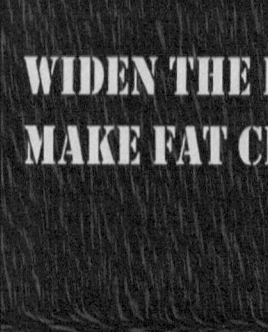 **WIDEN THE BOTTOM TO MAKE FAT CHEEKS**

CREATING A FACE FROM BASIC HEAD SHAPE

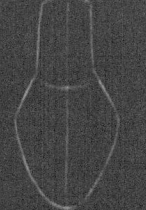

ALWAYS USE GUIDE-LINES

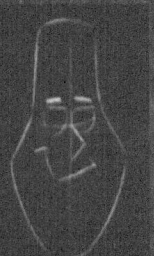

PLACE THE BRIDGE OF THE NOSE AT THE POINT WERE THE GUIDELINES INTERSECTS. PLACE THE EYE, OR GLASSES IN THIS CASE, EVENLY SPACED ON EITHER SIDE OF THE VERTICAL

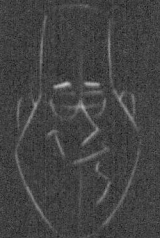

NOW WE WILL DRAW THE EARS, APPROXIMATELY THE HEIGHT OF THE EYES, AND ADD LOWER LIPS AND CHIN TO THE MOUTH AREA

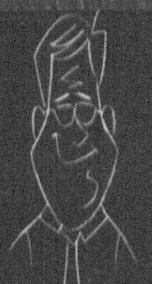

NOW ERASE ALL THE GUIDELINES ADD DETAILS HAIR, FOREHEAD WRINKELS, CLOTHES ETC ACCORDING TO YOUR STYLE,- JUST DONT OVER DO IT

Drawing Cartoon Head

We'll begin with th head because its the part of the body thats the most fun part to draw. when you start with tthe headyour character is almst ready,then we can work on facial expressions, body, motionand background.

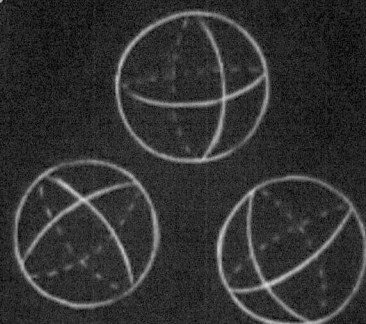

When drawing the head remember to think as a 3dimensional objects. try to draw the same .

The head is a bit more complex then a simple circle , make it simple and easy to do lets do it .

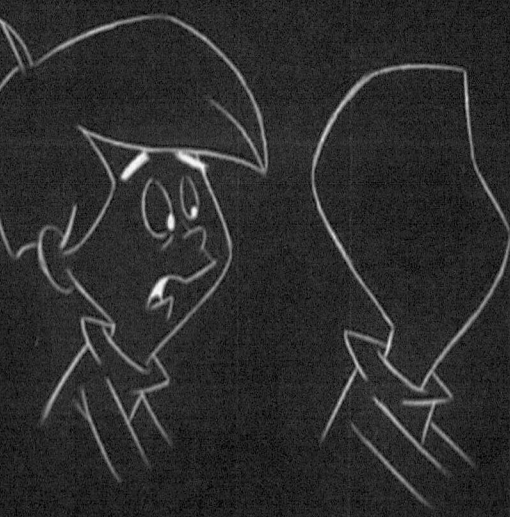

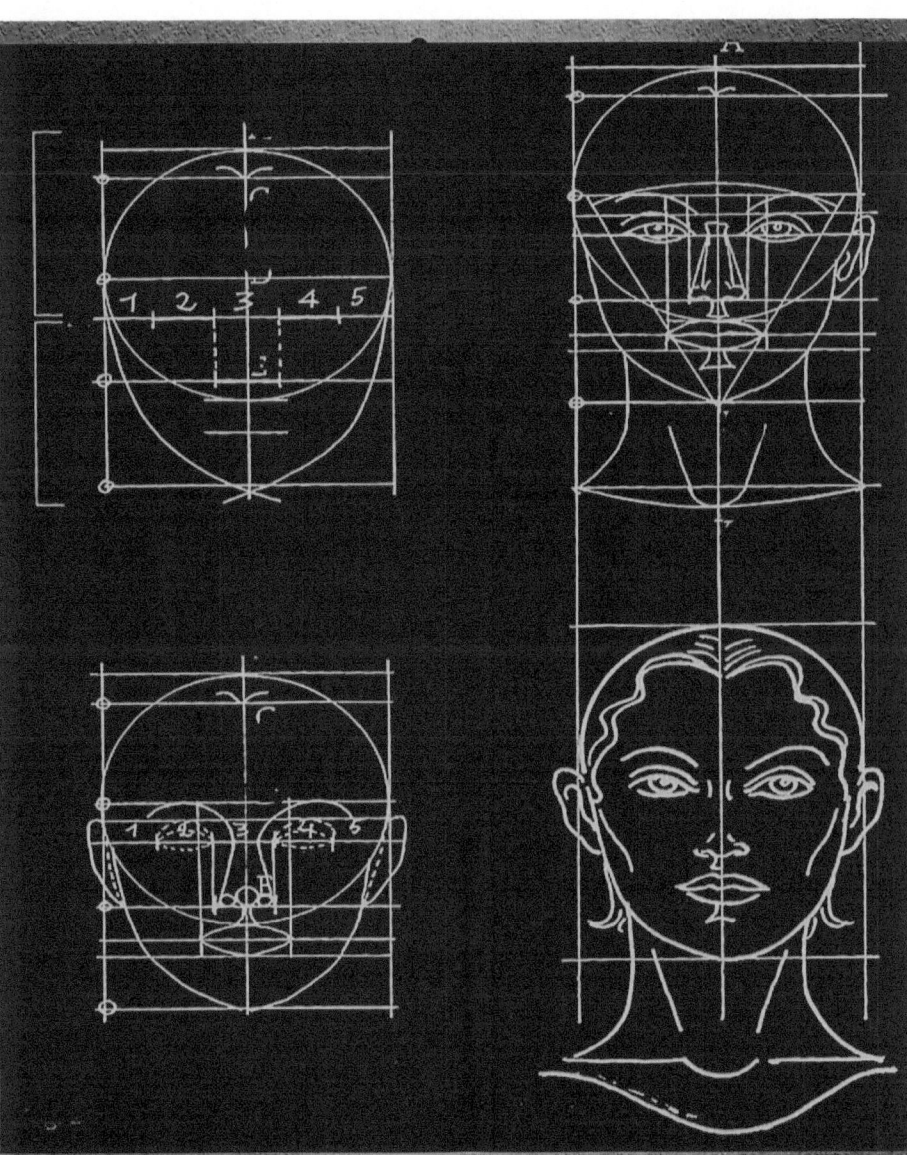

Always remember to draw guilde lines, this is box type guide lines divide a box into 4 boxes in equal size and place the eyes, lips, nose according to your character.

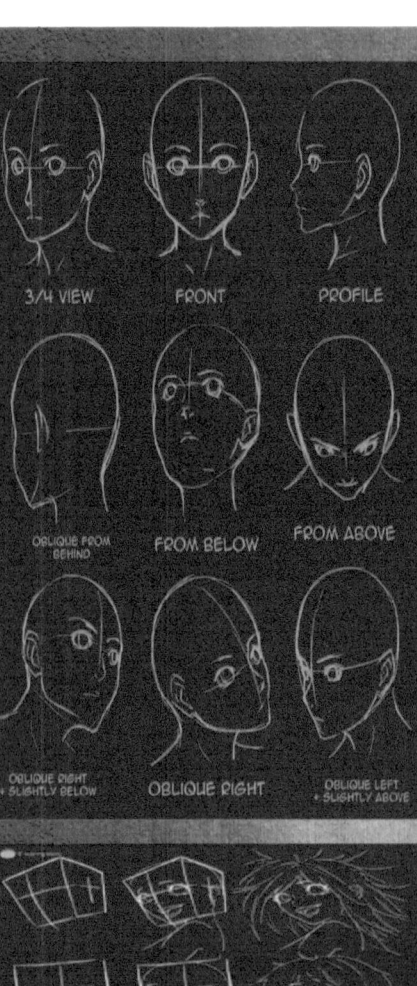
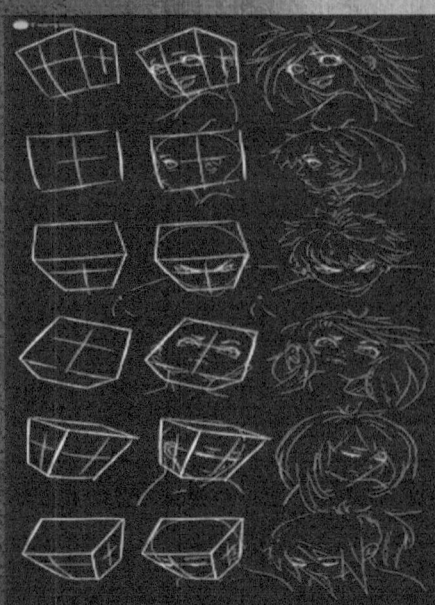
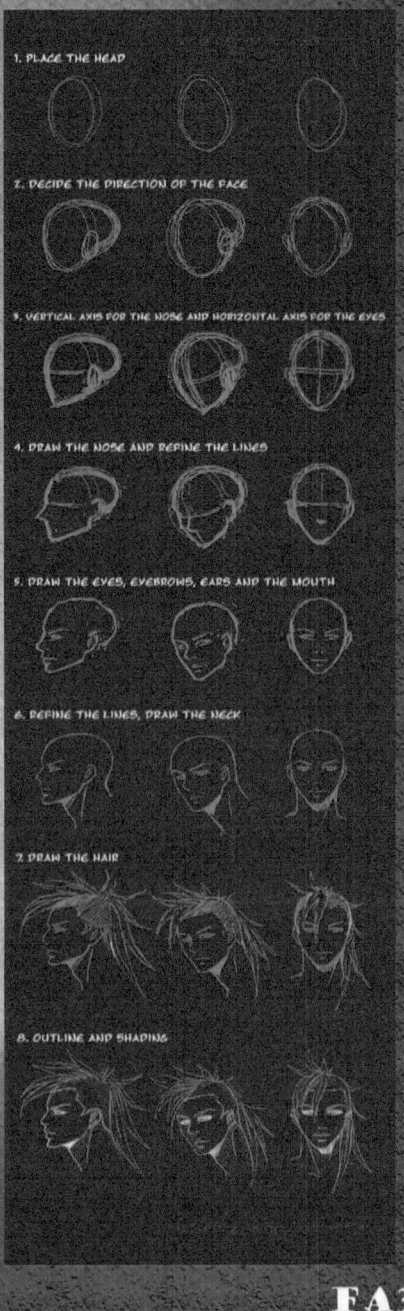

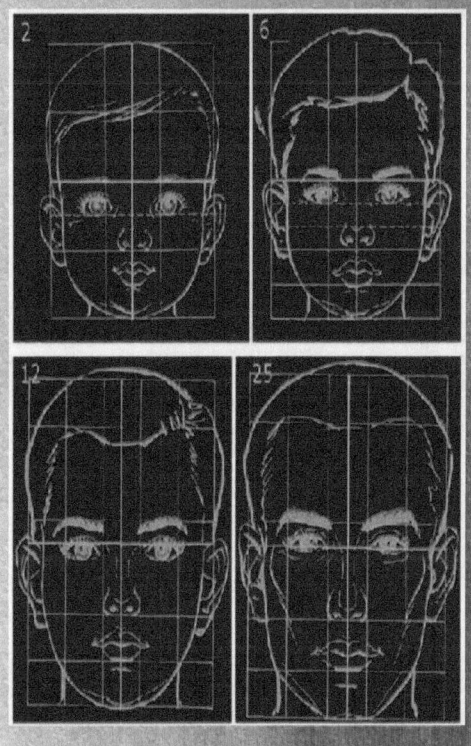

if u notice as the cha-rater get older his forehead get bigger and the centre line goes lower

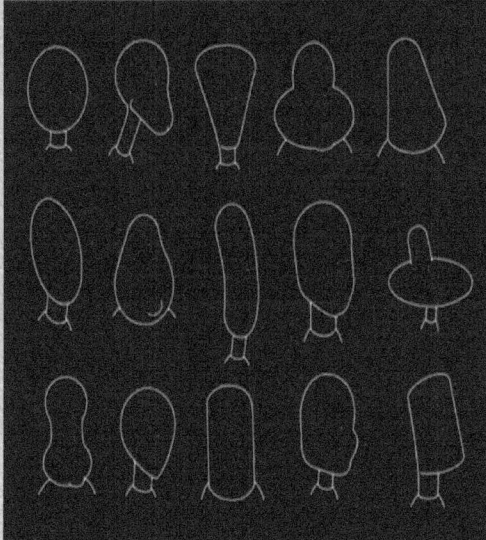

once you understand the face structure you can customize your own cartoon

FA3

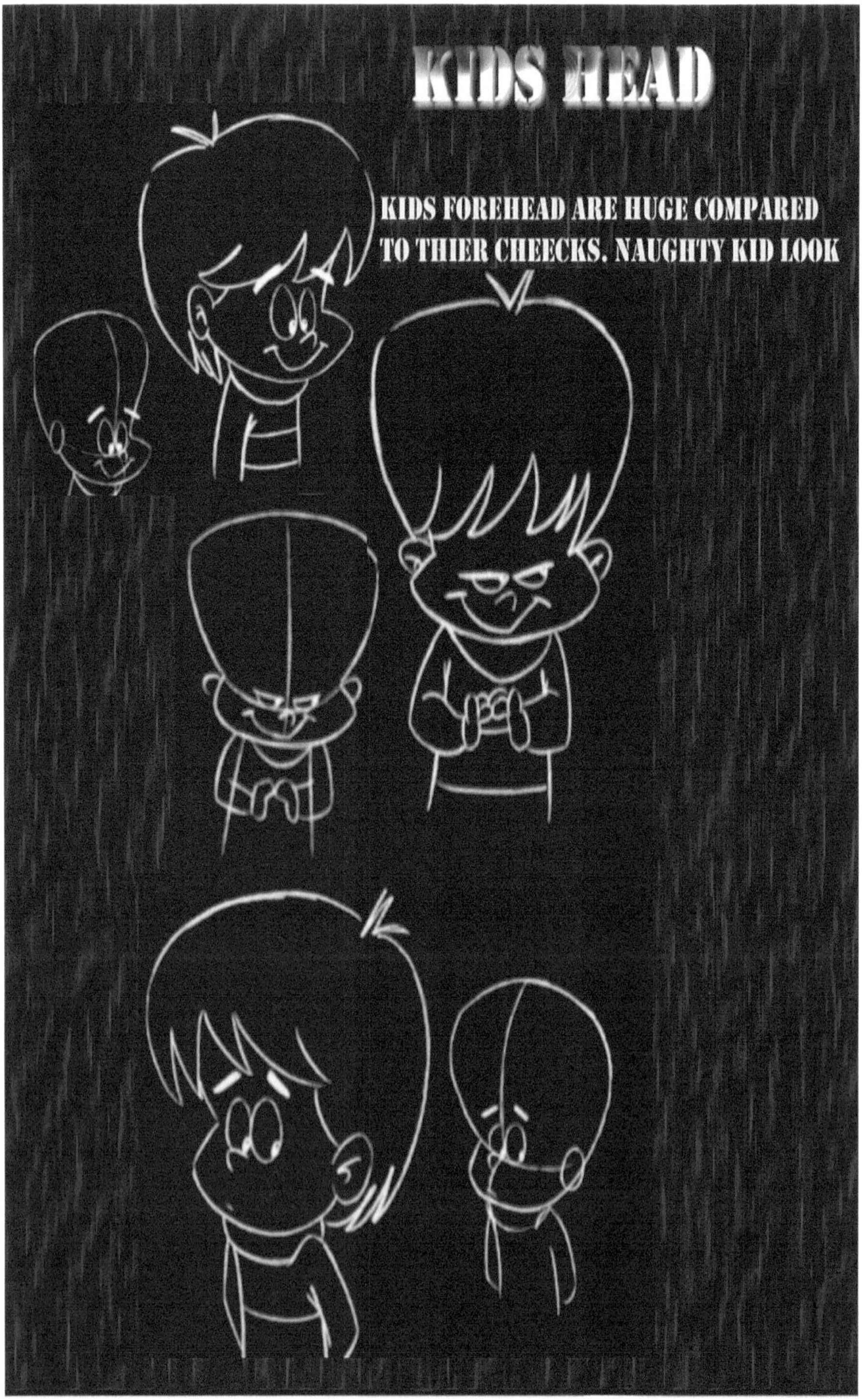

KIDS HEAD

KIDS FOREHEAD ARE HUGE COMPARED TO THIER CHEECKS. NAUGHTY KID LOOK

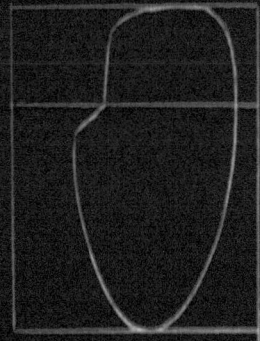
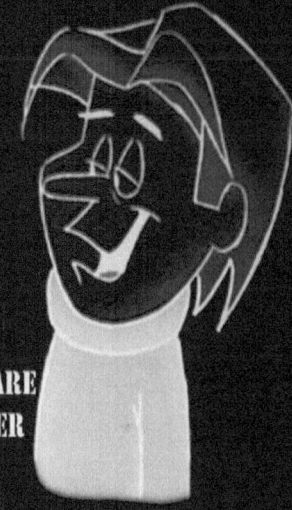

EVERY AGE GROUP CHARACTERSTICS ARE DIFFERENT THE OLDER THE CHARACTER SMALLER THE FOREHEAD

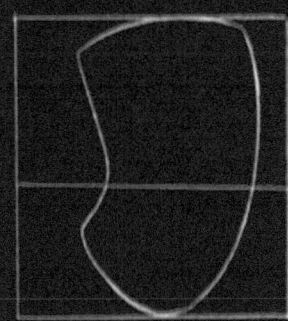
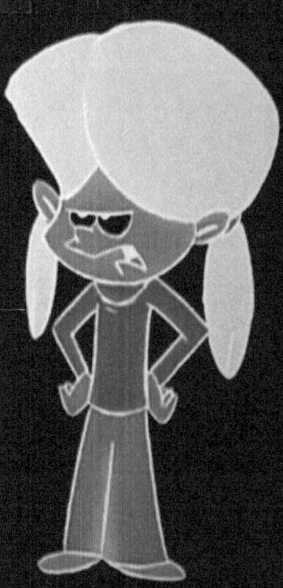

EYES ARE PLACED HIGHER ON HIS HEAD FOR OLDER CHARACTER'S

FEW MORE SAMPLES FOR YOUR CARTOON CHARACTER HEADS

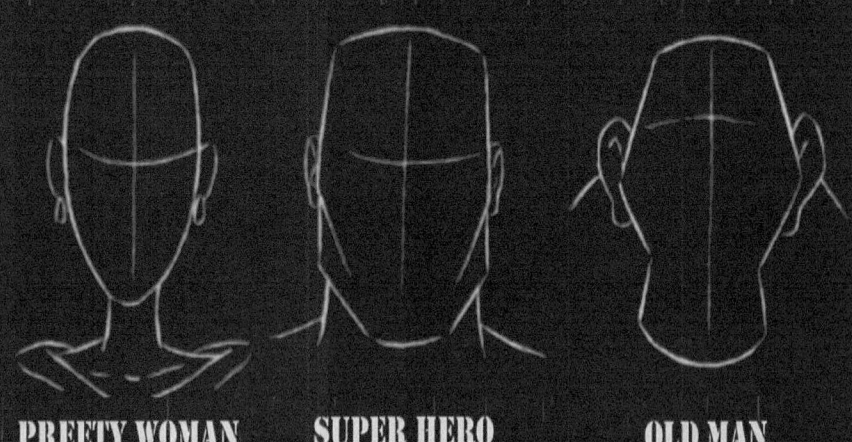

PREETY WOMAN   SUPER HERO   OLD MAN

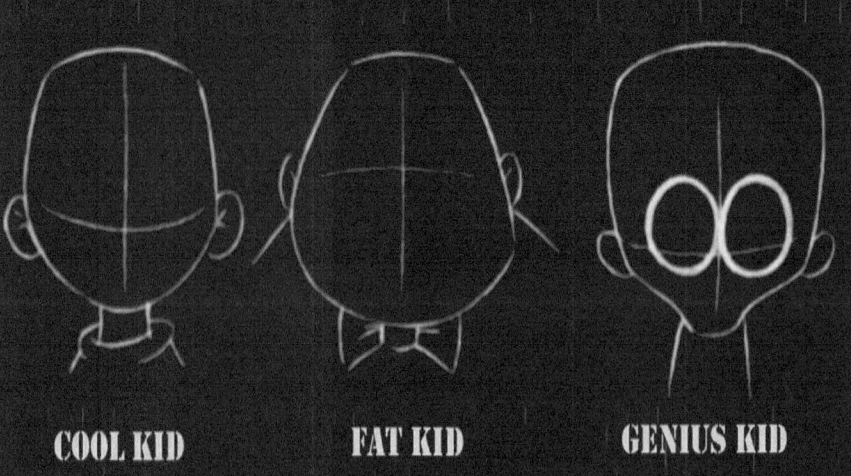

COOL KID   FAT KID   GENIUS KID

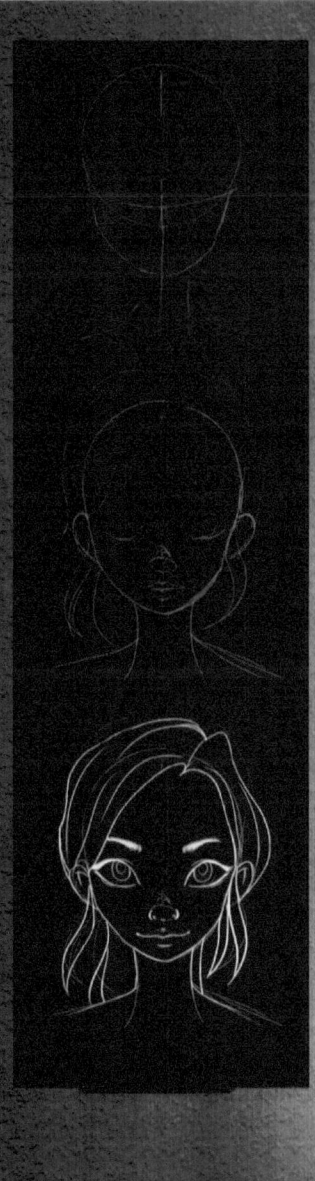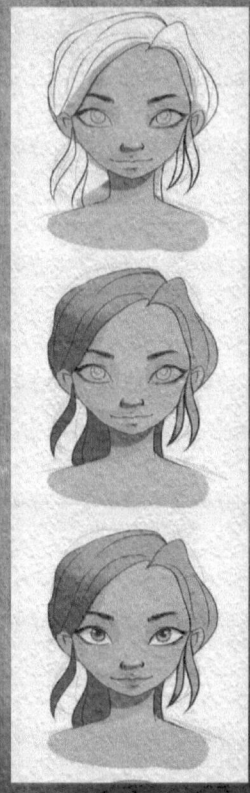

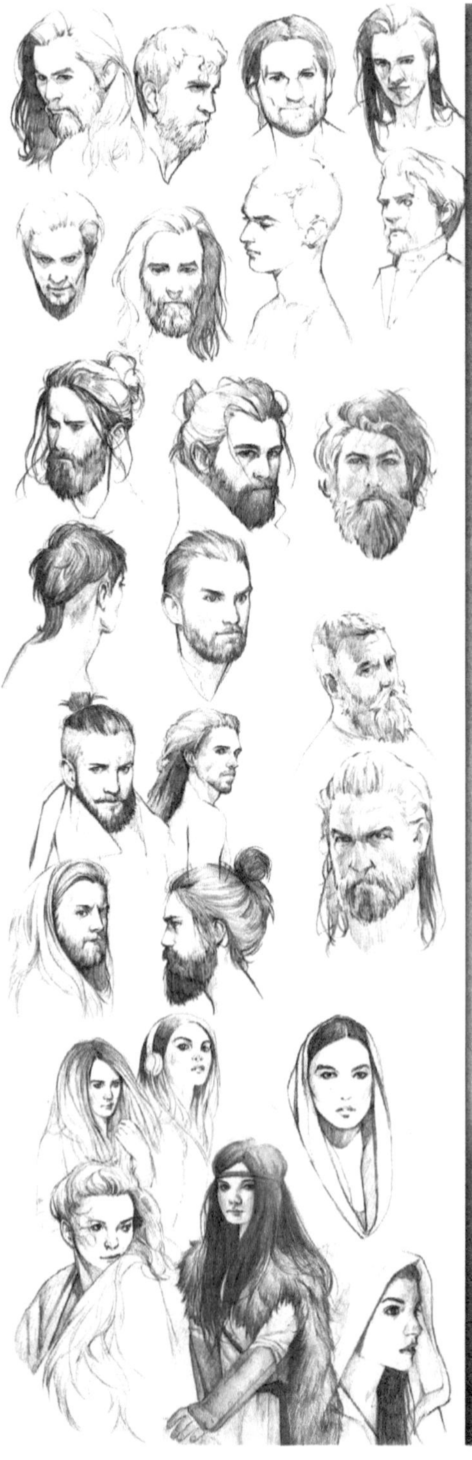

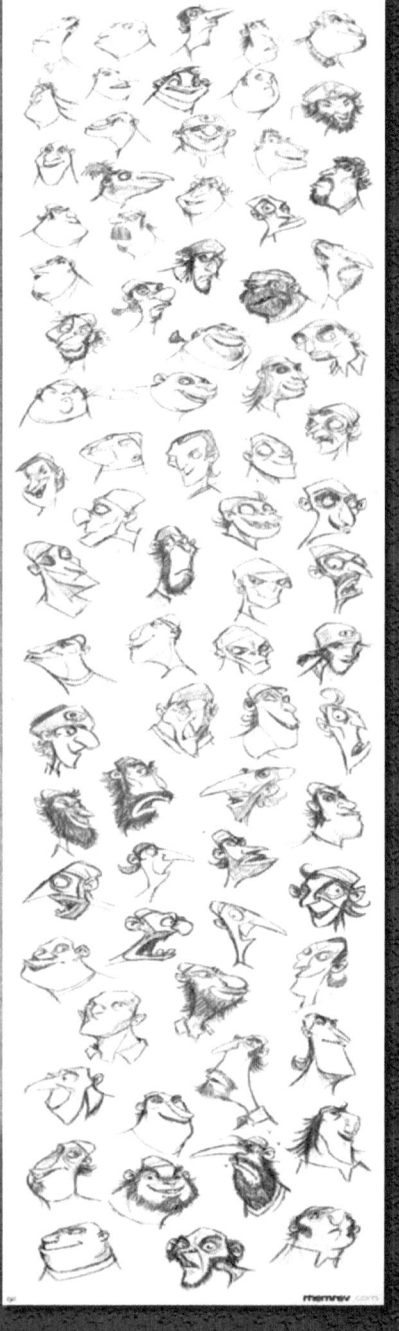

FA3

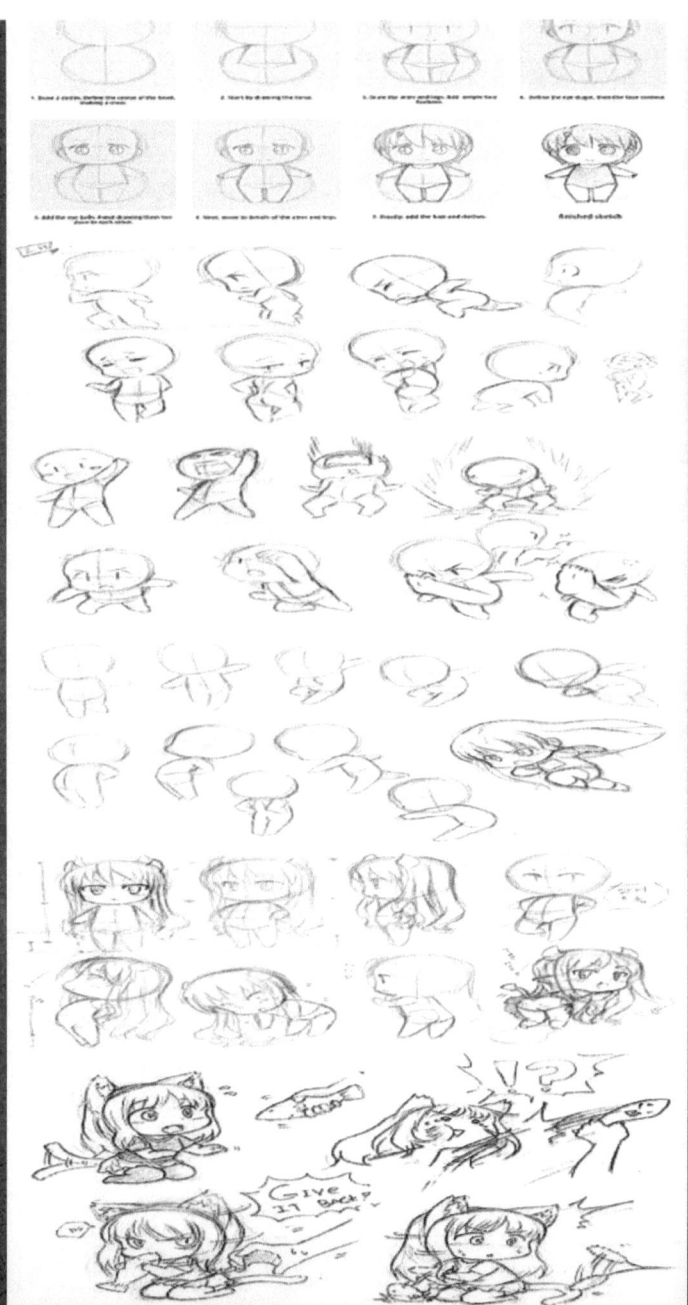

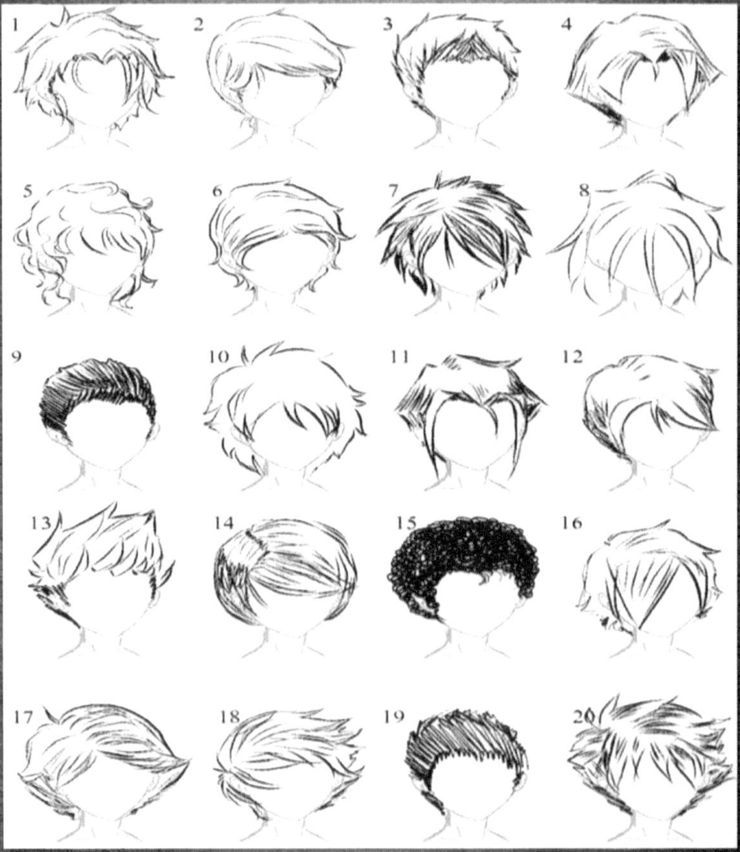

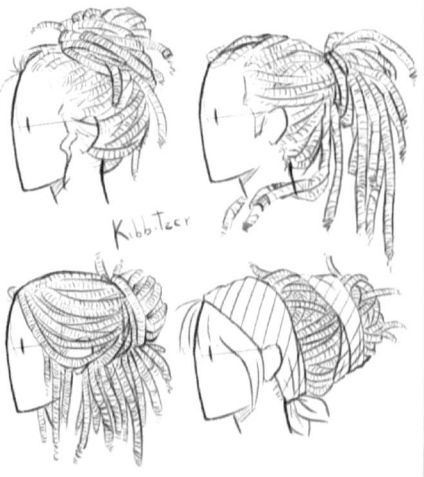

Some samples of hair styles for your charaters always try new stlyes dont stop your imginations try all stlyes

FA3

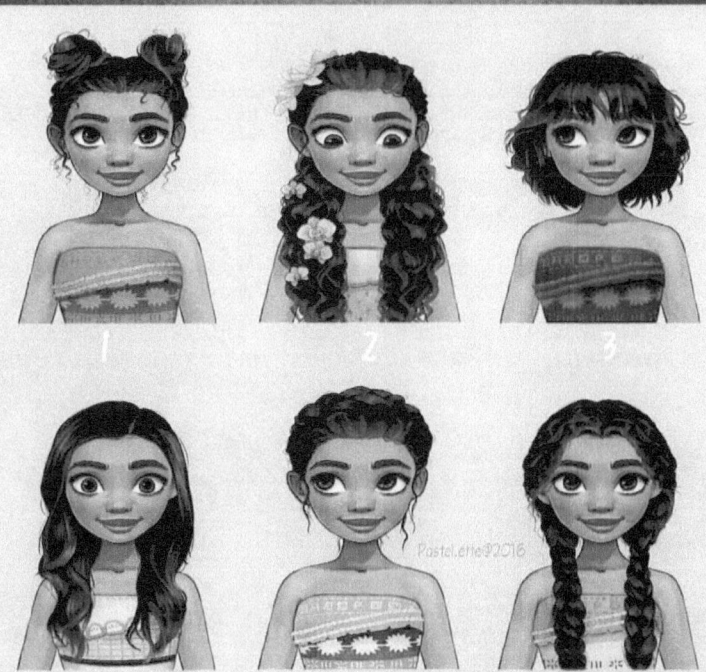

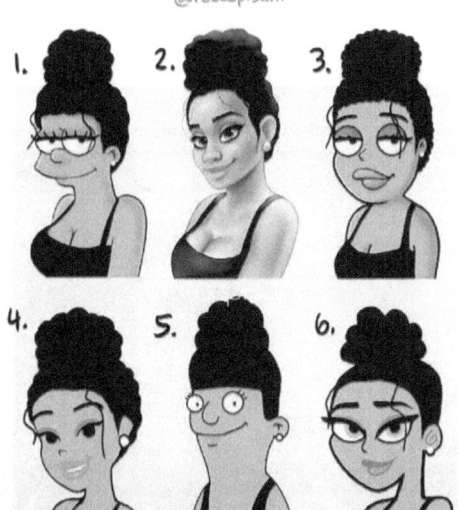

Try to copy this artistist ideas and cutomize your charaters onces you get used to it, try to do charaters from real life

FA3

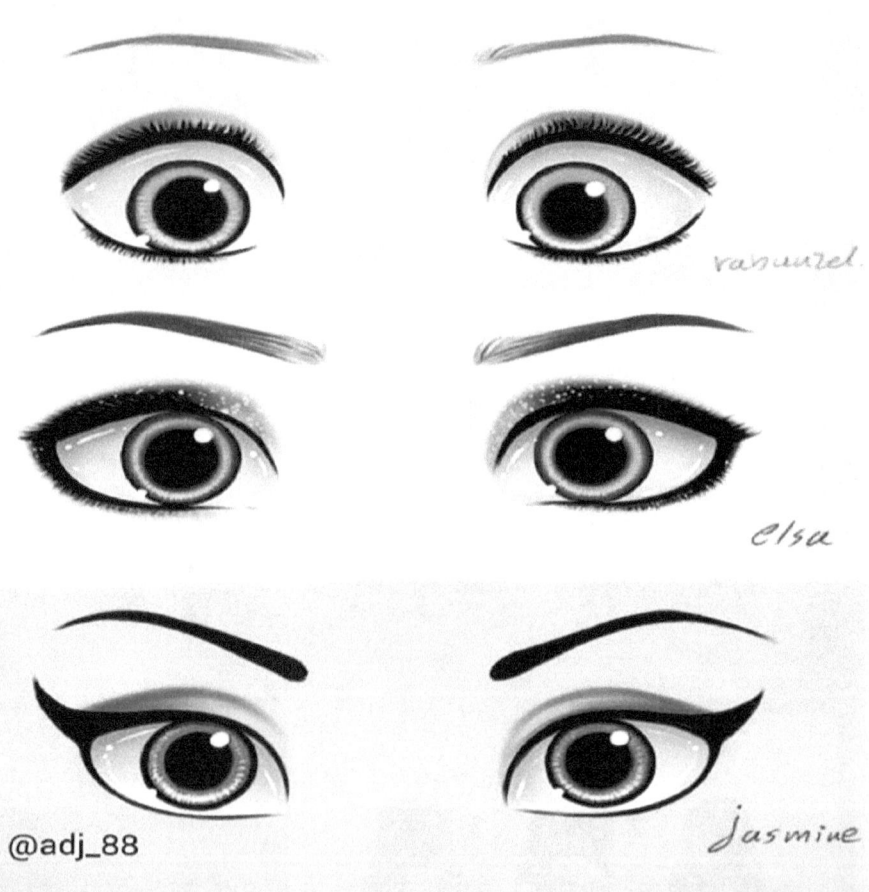

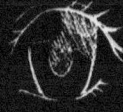
Start out by drawing a curve. This is the upper eyelash-line.

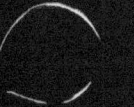
Coloured it...

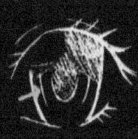
Then add the lower curve. This one is smaller than the upper.

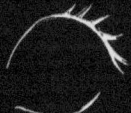
Then a few lines to give the eye depth.

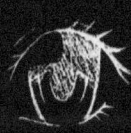
Add eyelashes seperately. You decide how many and how thick/long they should be.

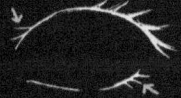
Starting at the middle and going down, I made a gradient shading - by pressing hard in the beginning and then easening the pressure downward.

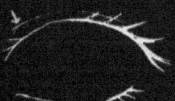
A few more lashes, also on the bottom line.

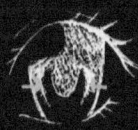
Again, now just smaller and darker than the first one - to give more depth.

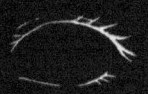
Then add the eyelid line(s).

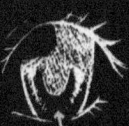
Then I added a few sharp lines to give the iris some structure.

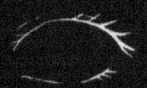
Remember the eyebrows! Many beginners tend to forget them, even though the brows are an important part of the expression.

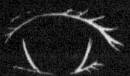
Add the highlight(s). The bigger and the more, the girlier the character will look.

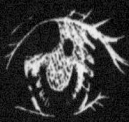
If you want, you can use an eraser to make some more light effects/highlights.

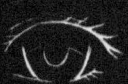
Now draw the iris. Big irises look more intense than small ones.

The circle in the middle is the pupil, and I surrounded it by some more shades, but you can choose just to make a full circle instead.

FA3

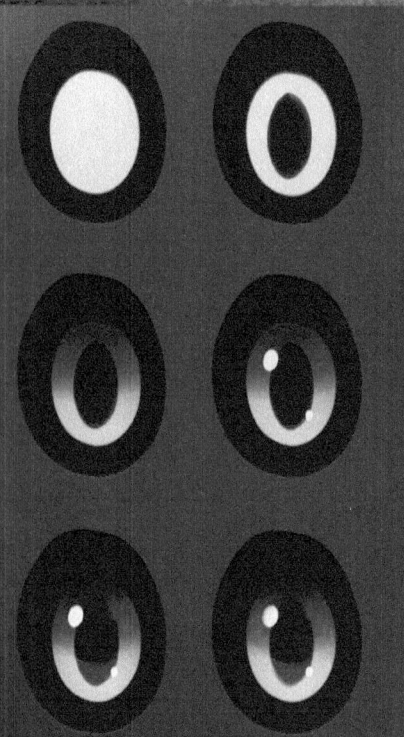

Start with circle shade according to light reflection, where you see white tiny circle that is according to the light

Begin with a simple wide open eye shape and a pupil, afterwards paint over a smooth base shadow wich usually covers a half of the eye coming from top down. Two bright spots - a direct reflection from the brightest light sources... after that paint in more yet less bright reflections and details to make it look more realistic.

Remember, all the reflections depends on environment - the count of reflections, position, angle and brightness. Eye also reflects different specular colours which also just adds to realism. Also, experiment and see if you get an unexpected fun results which doesn't have to have all 'by the book'.

FA3

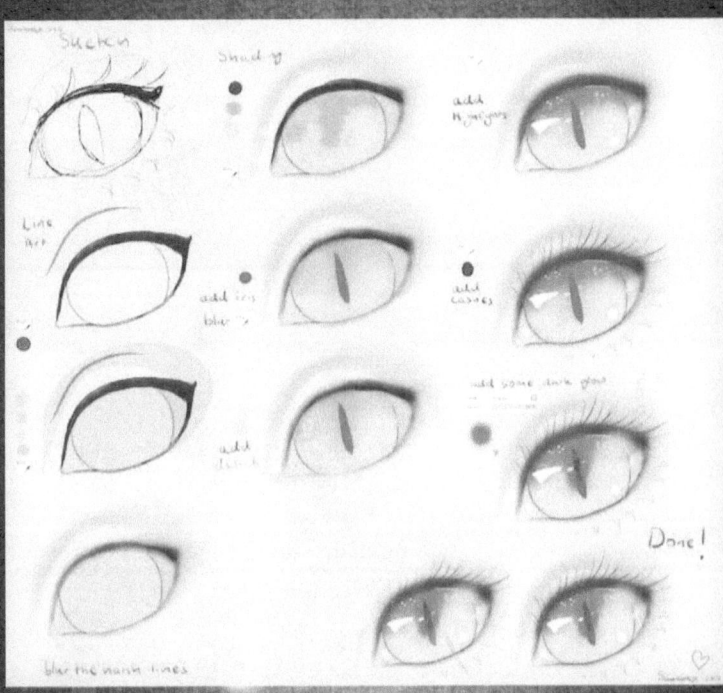
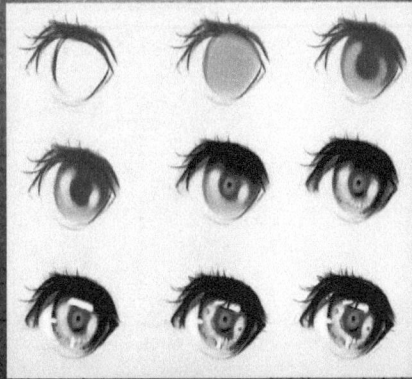

Every line you draw counts it makes it a shade darker and thicker

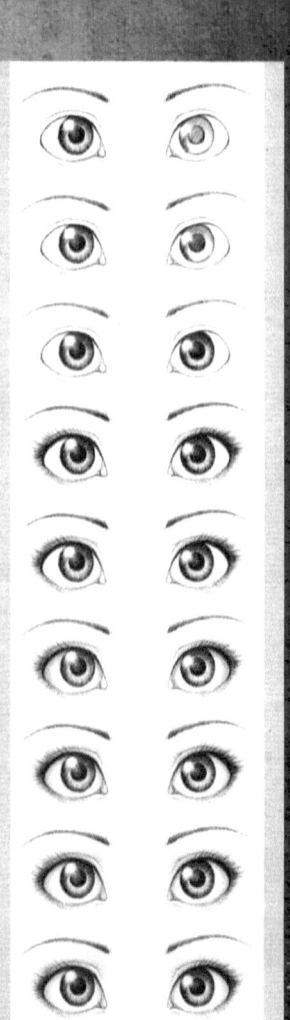

Few samples you can try add to your cartoon, mix match do experiments till you become perfect

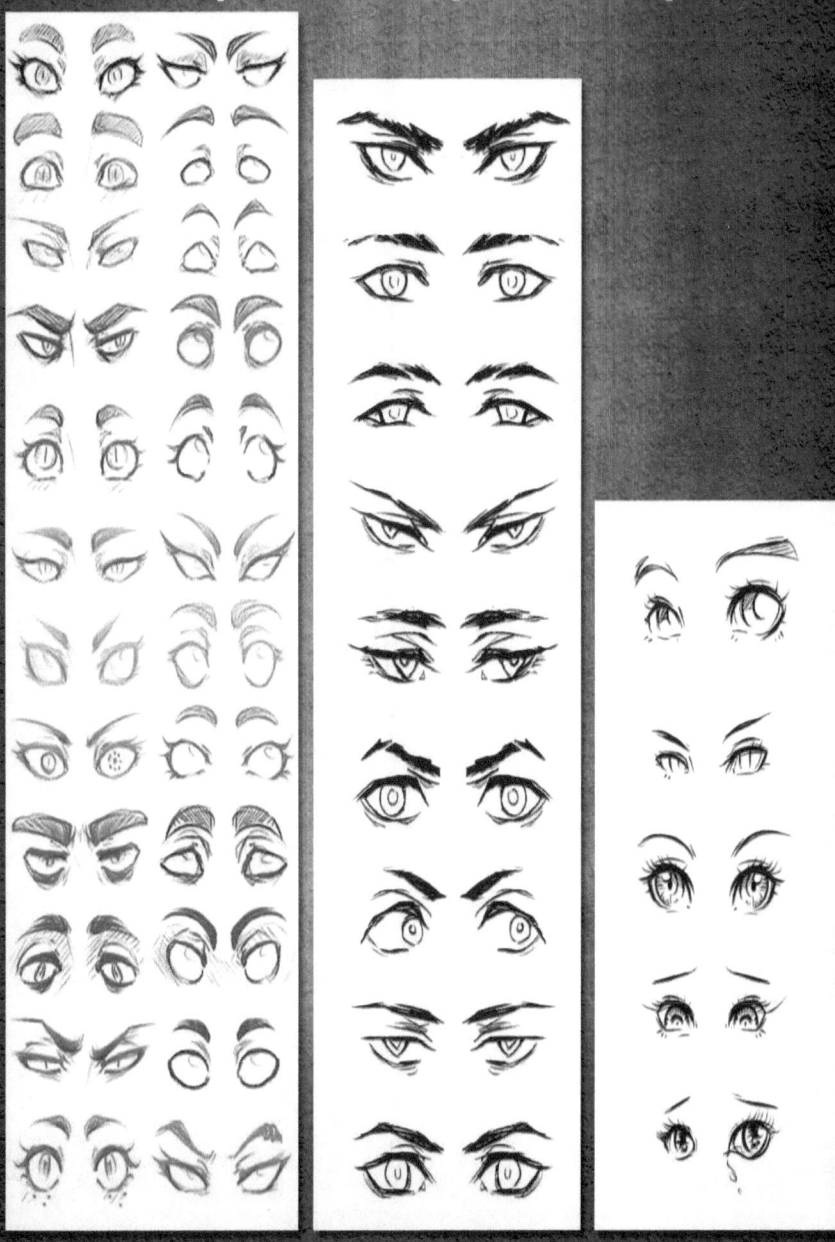

FA3

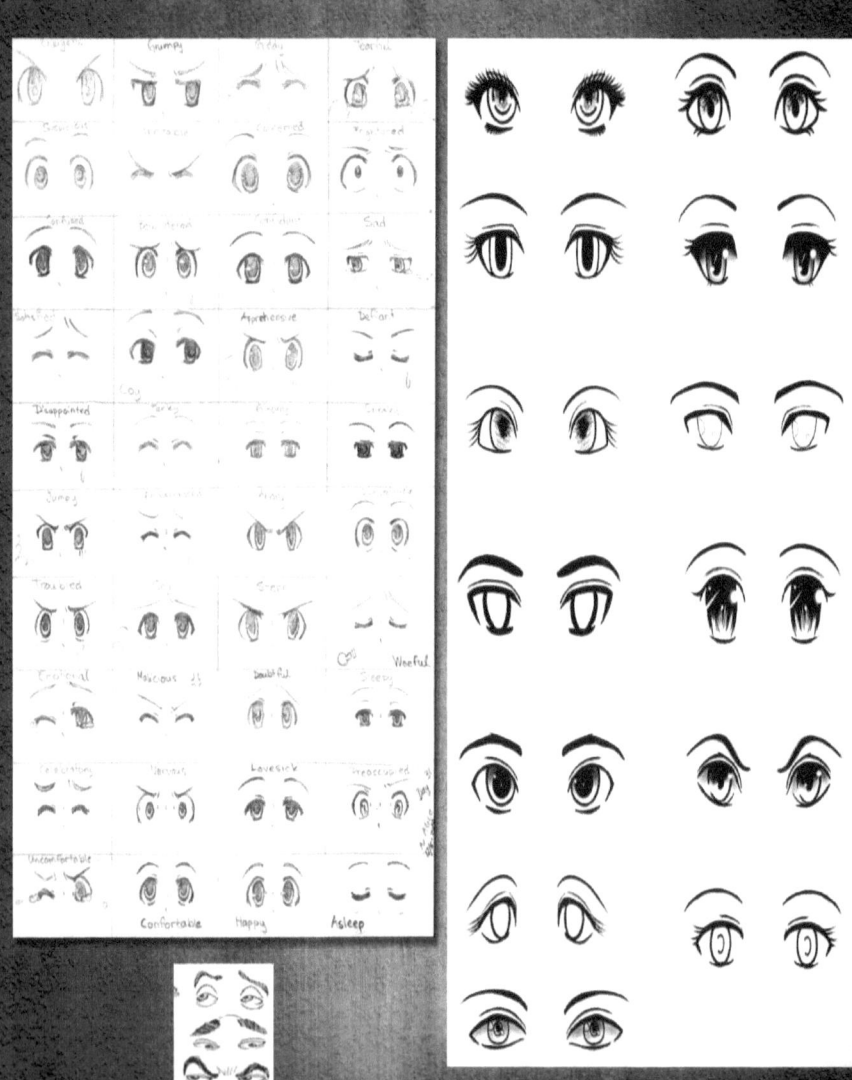

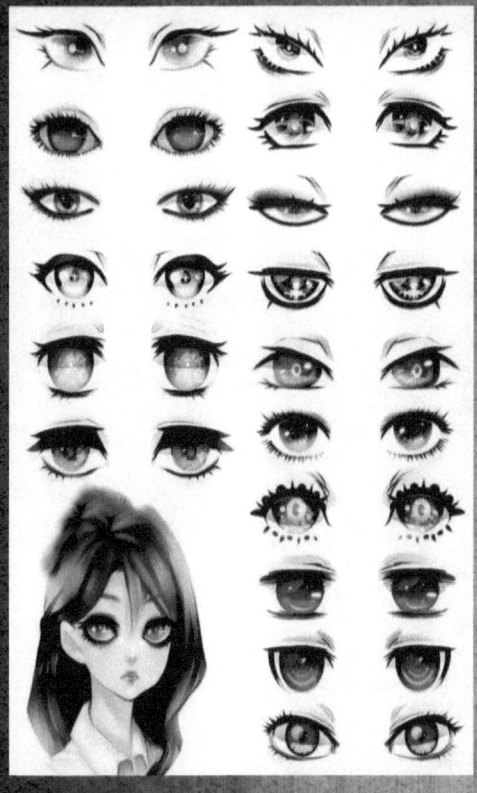
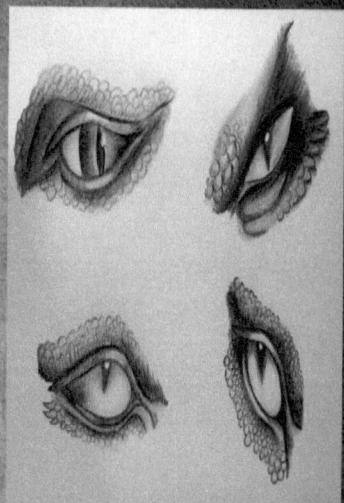
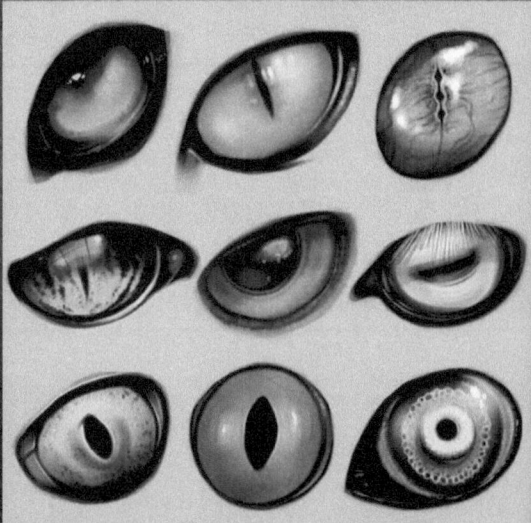

HOW TO DRAW:
The Nose

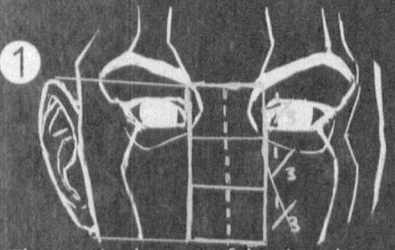

The nose is a key part of drawing a human face. It gives depth to our otherwise flat faces, and holds tremendous potential for character. However, it is often that they are skewed and awkwardly placed due to a lack of understanding of a few basic concepts. First, know the limits of the nose.

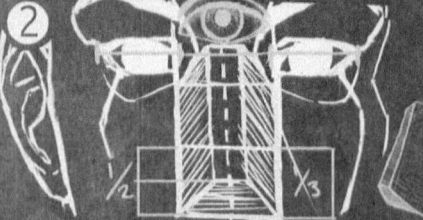

Block in a trapezoid prism, which is key to keep the nose oriented in space and structurally right. Remember that the nose is about the same width as an eye, and as tall as the middle third of the face, sharing the same height as the ears.

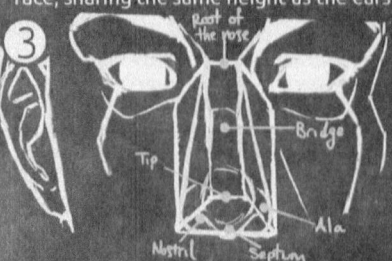

The root of the nose lies above the eye-line, starting skinny at the root, and widening as it reaches the bottom, coming to a round tip, more or less. Recognize all the different parts of the nose, being aware of their relationship to surrounding features.

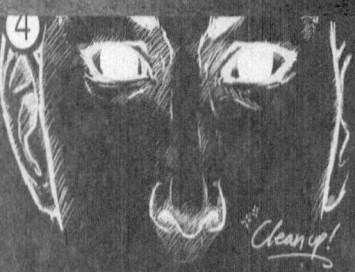

Add textures and sub-surface scattering to really bring out the structural beauty of the nose, bringing warm colors to it to bring your character to life.

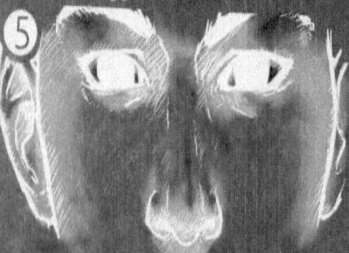

All noses are different and uniquely shaped, so this is just a standard. Noses can be perky, sculpted, bulby, broken, eagle-like, etc. Make sure to play around with different variations to get the character you want.

If you find this tutorial helpful, fav it and comment! Feel free to browse through my gallery or request stuff. Thank you :)

soas95.deviantart.com

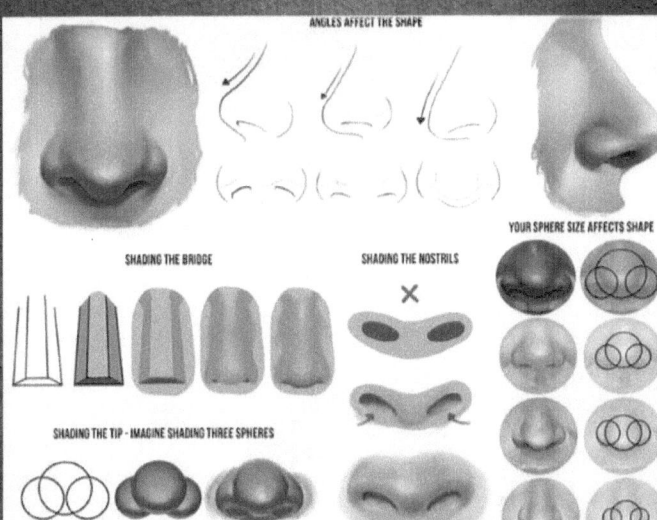
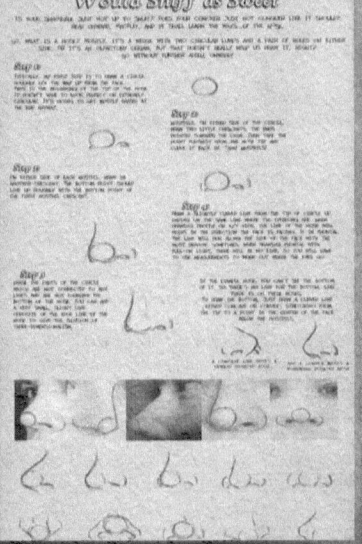
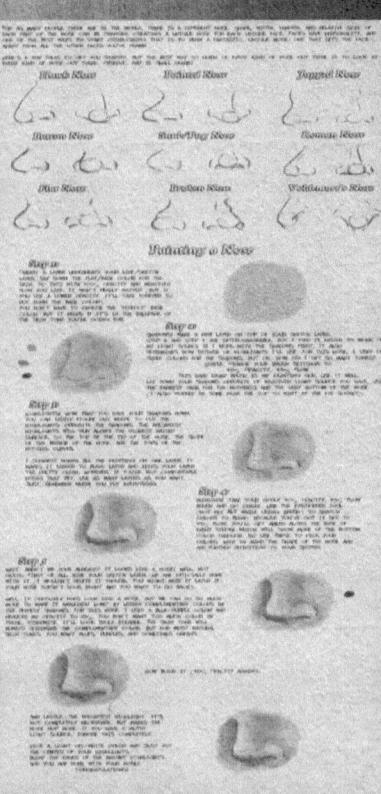

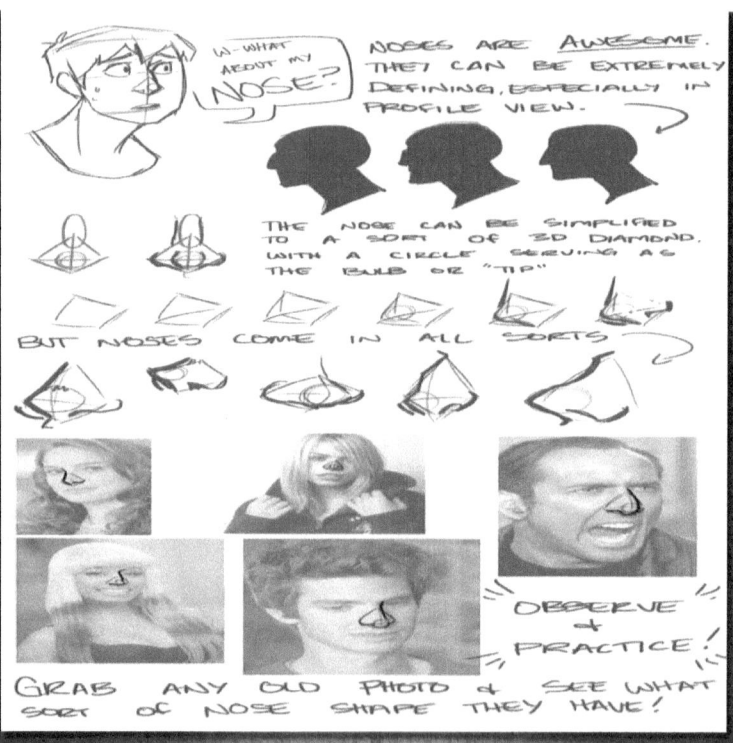
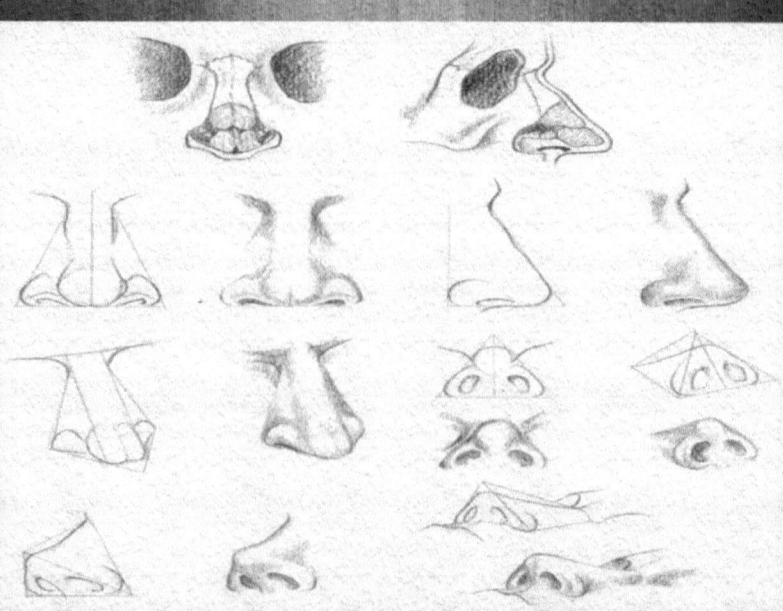

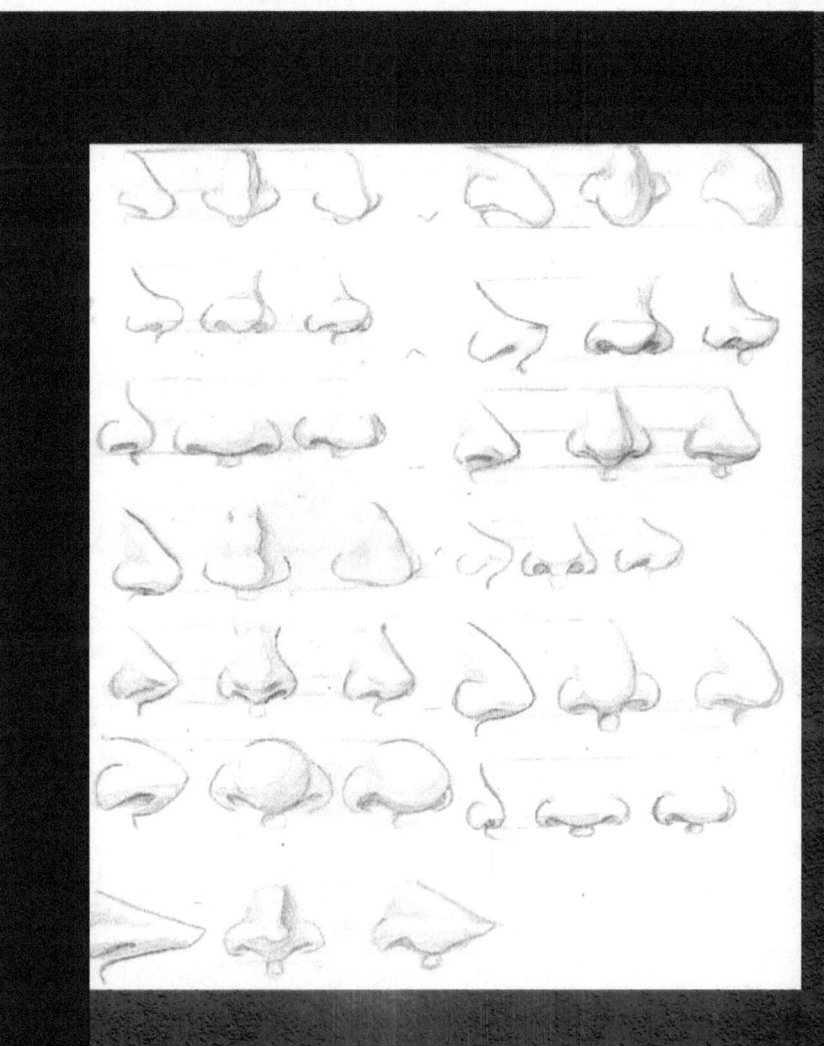

When you learn the basics struture you create best cartoons

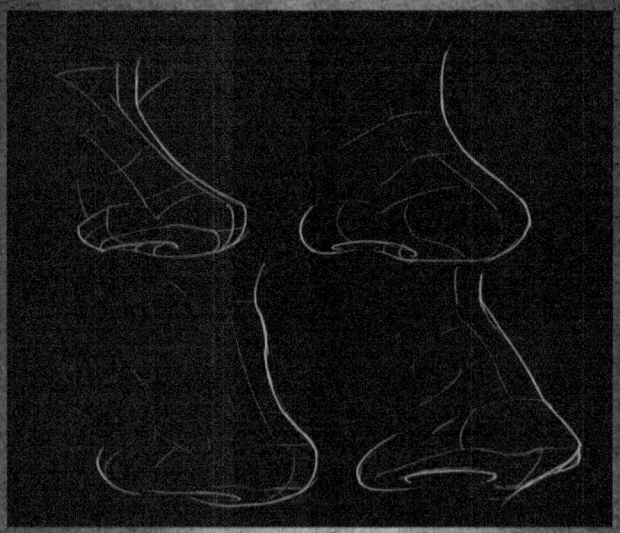

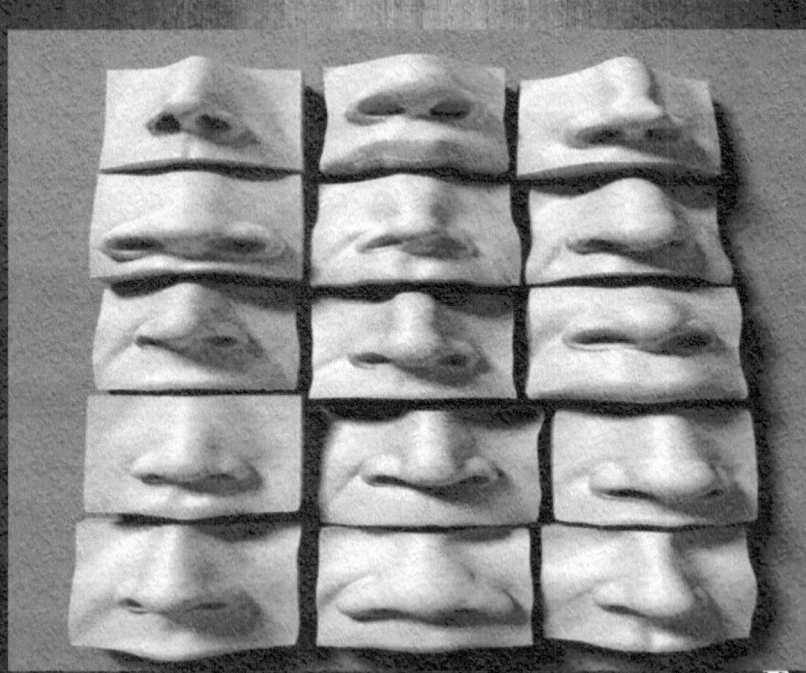

DRAWING LIPS

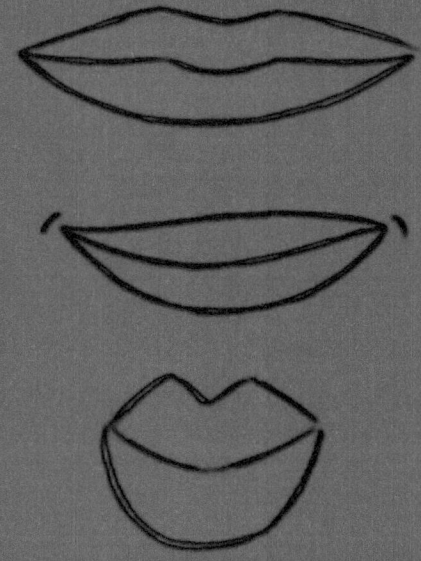

Classic woman lips

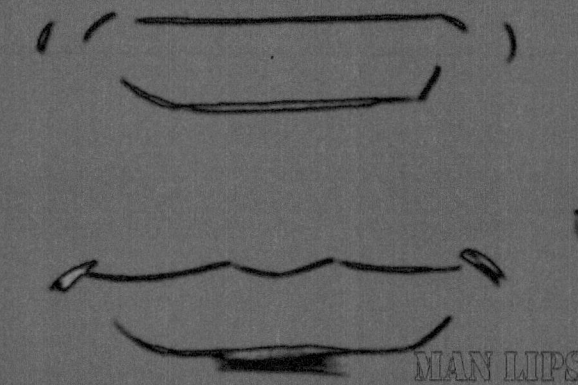

MAN LIPS

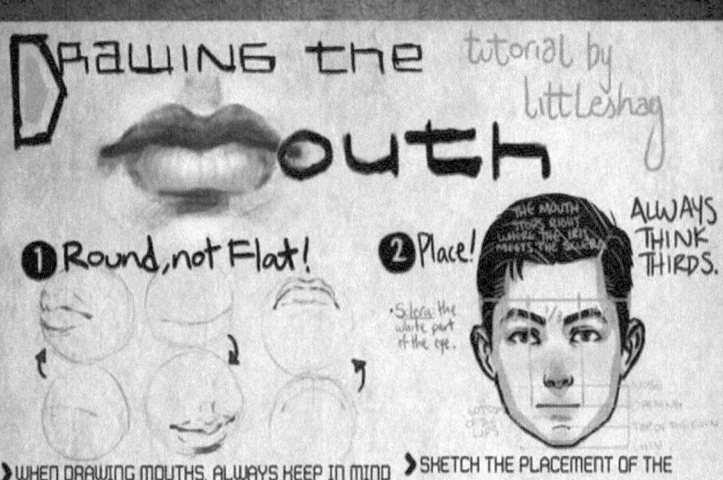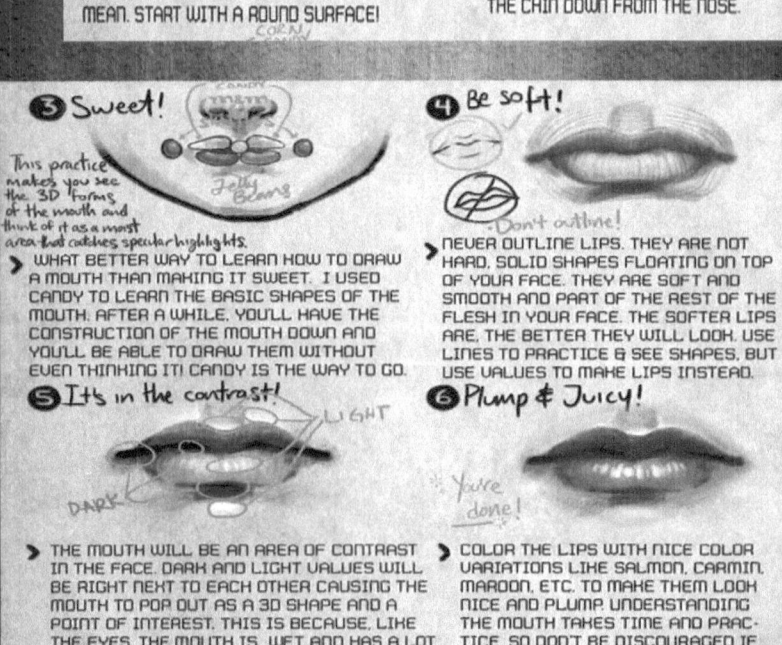

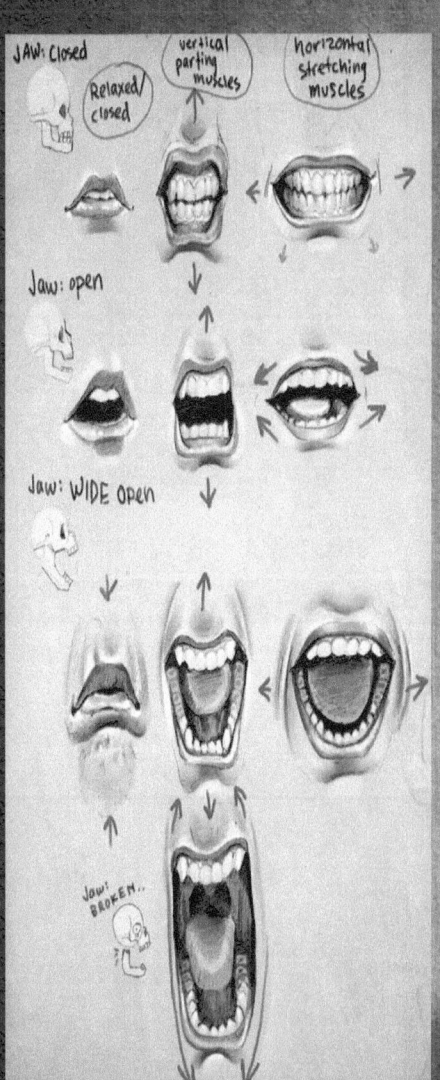
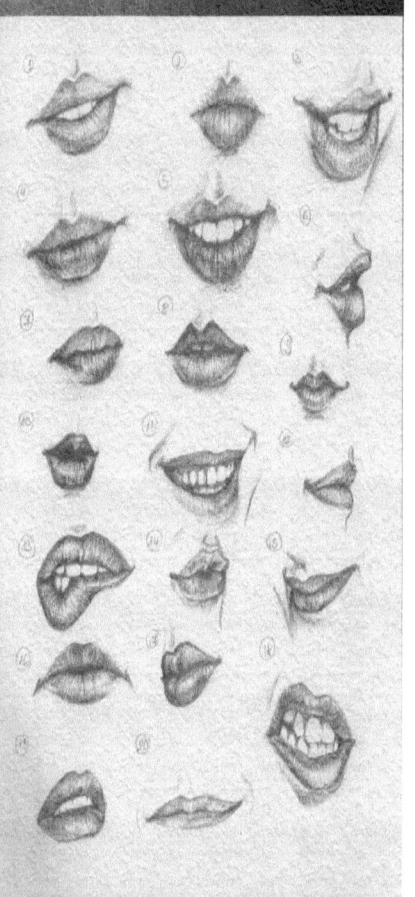

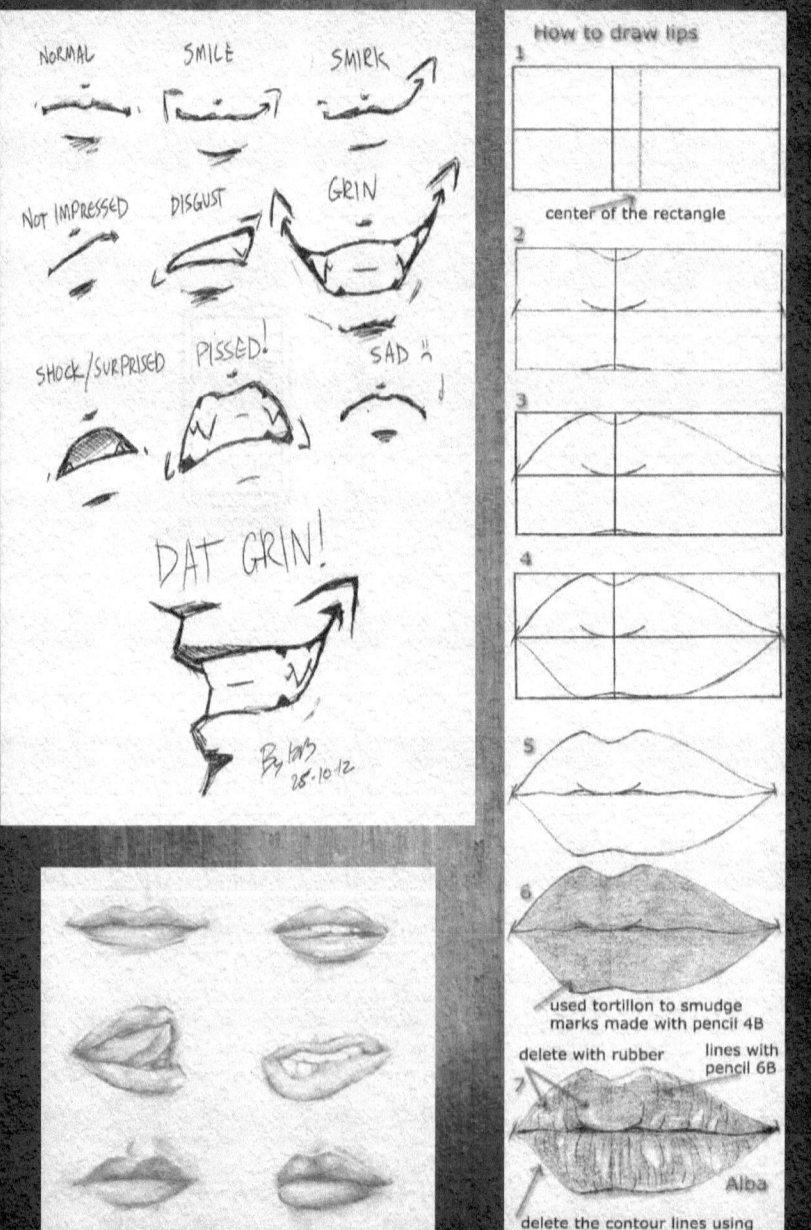

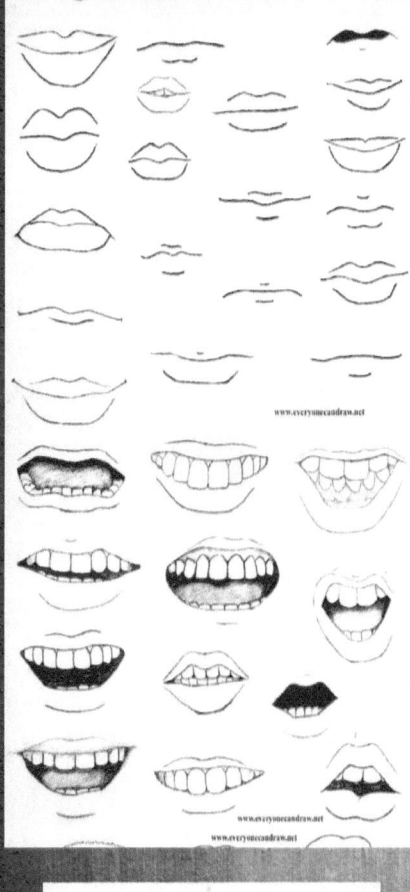
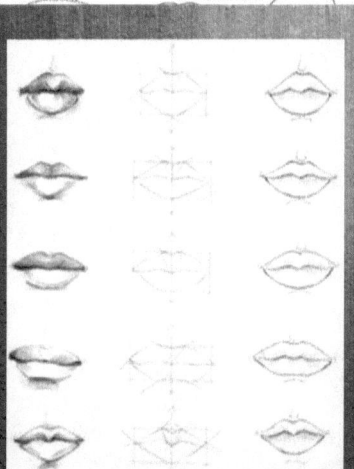

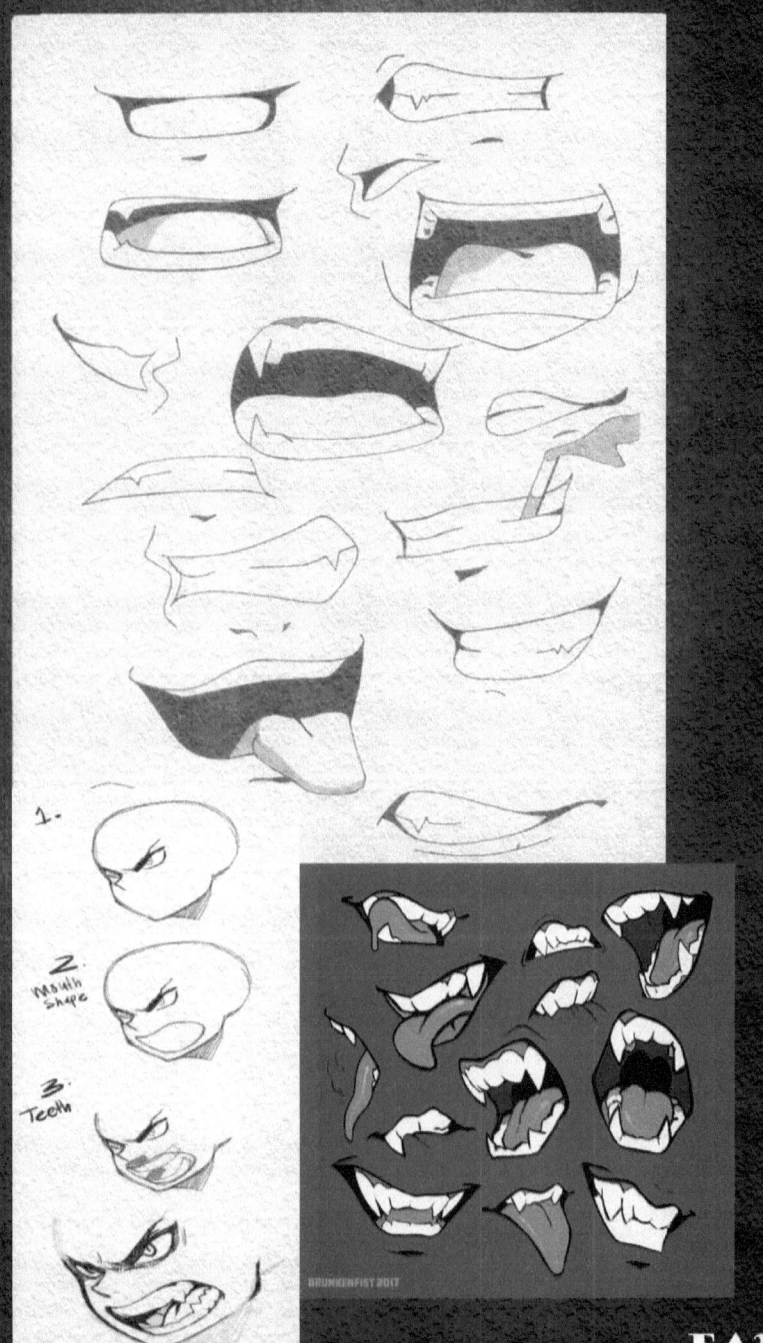

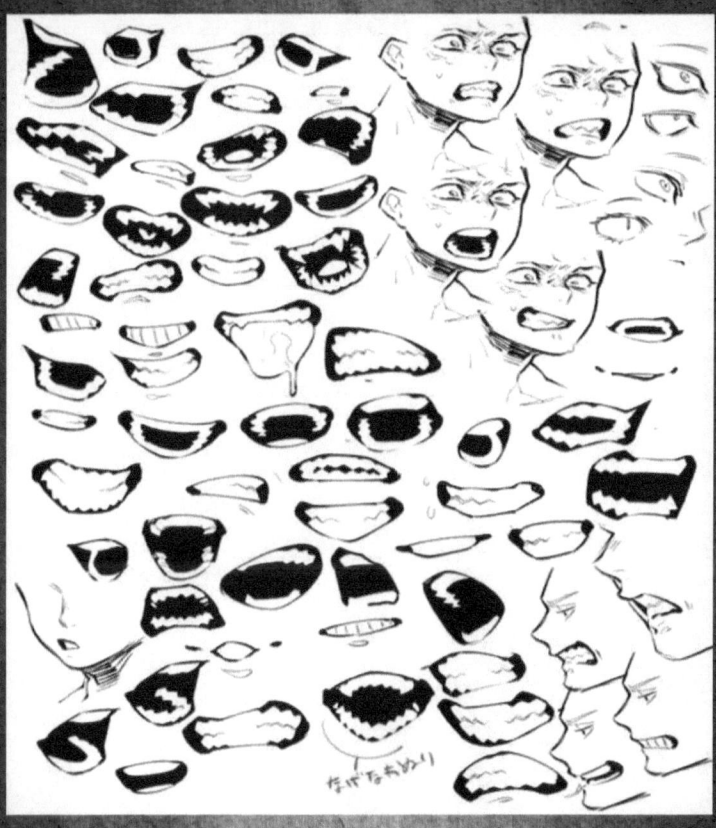
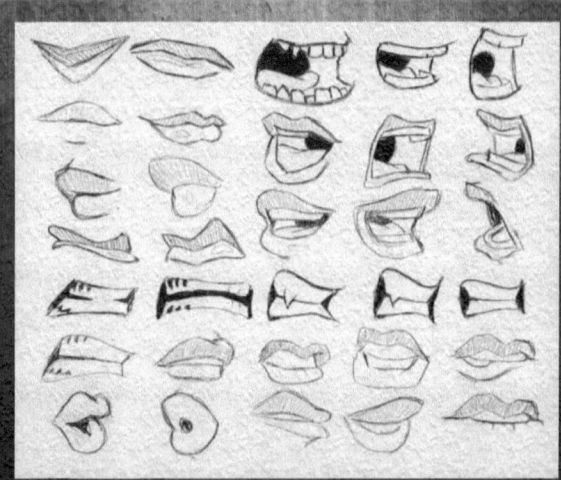

FA3

Teeth

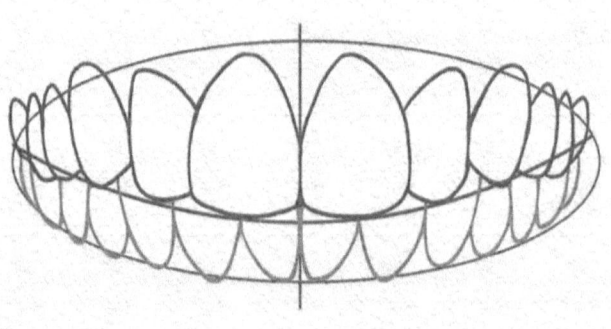

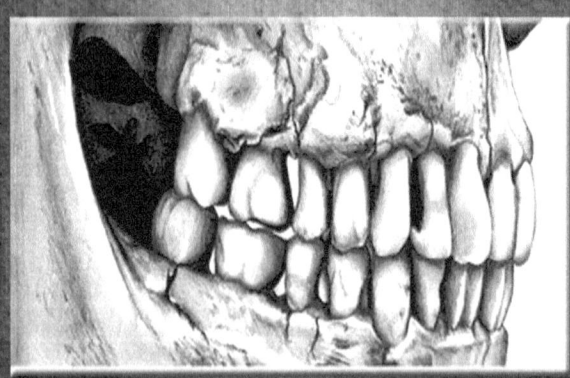

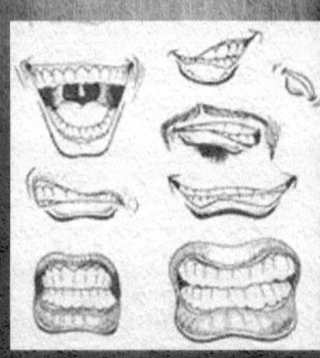

Teeth

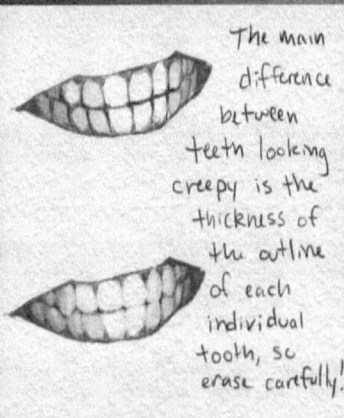

The main difference between teeth looking creepy is the thickness of the outline of each individual tooth, so erase carefully!

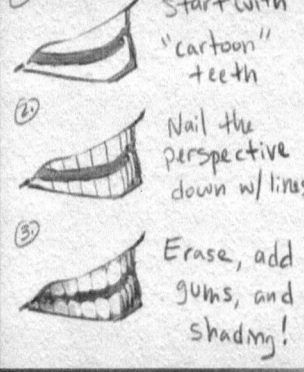

1. Start with "cartoon" teeth
2. Nail the perspective down w/ lines
3. Erase, add gums, and shading!

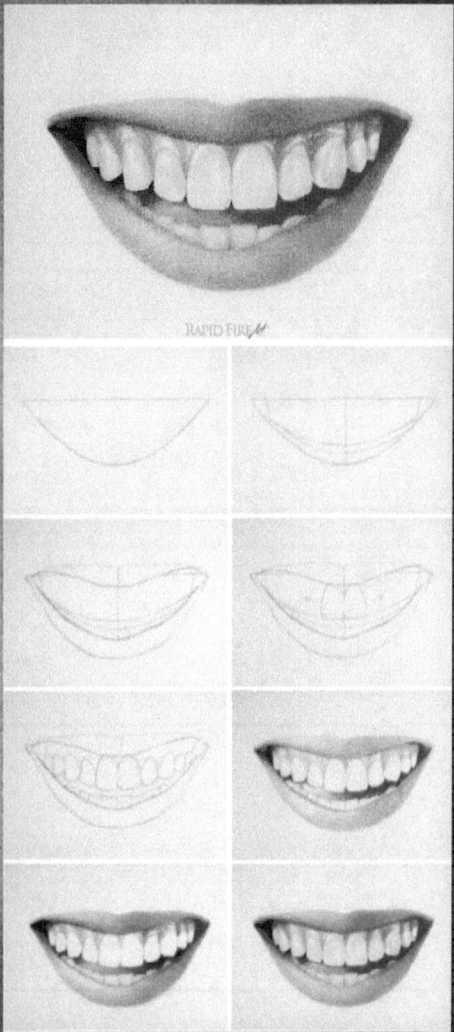

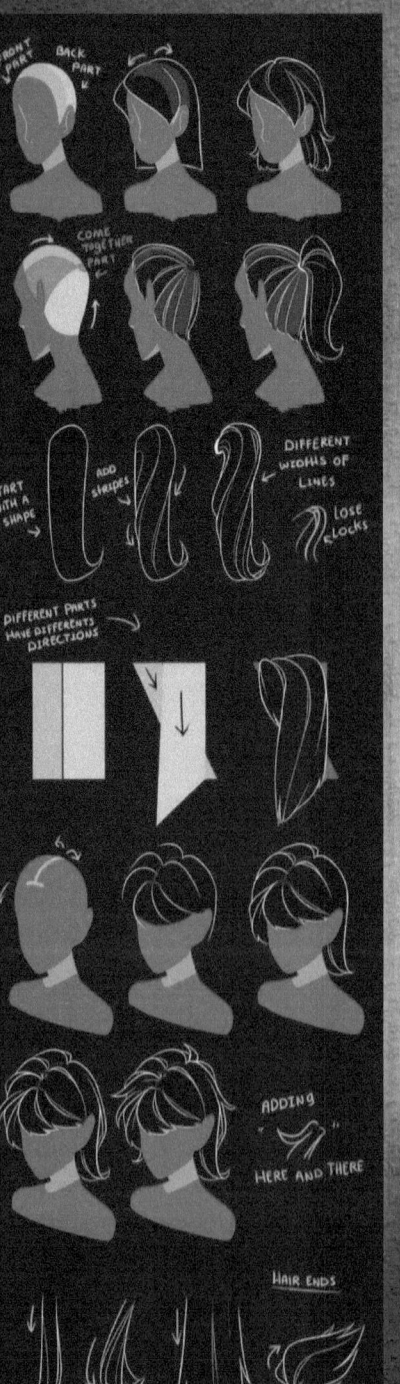

Hair can be tricky if you dont fellow the flow so fellow the direction of the flow. Every lines is a hair which has diferent volume of shades

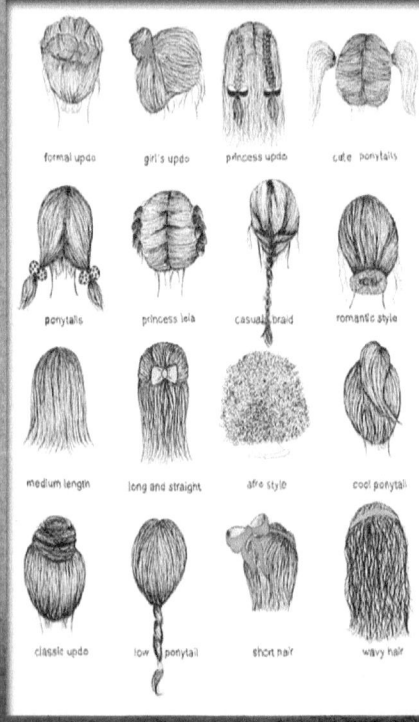

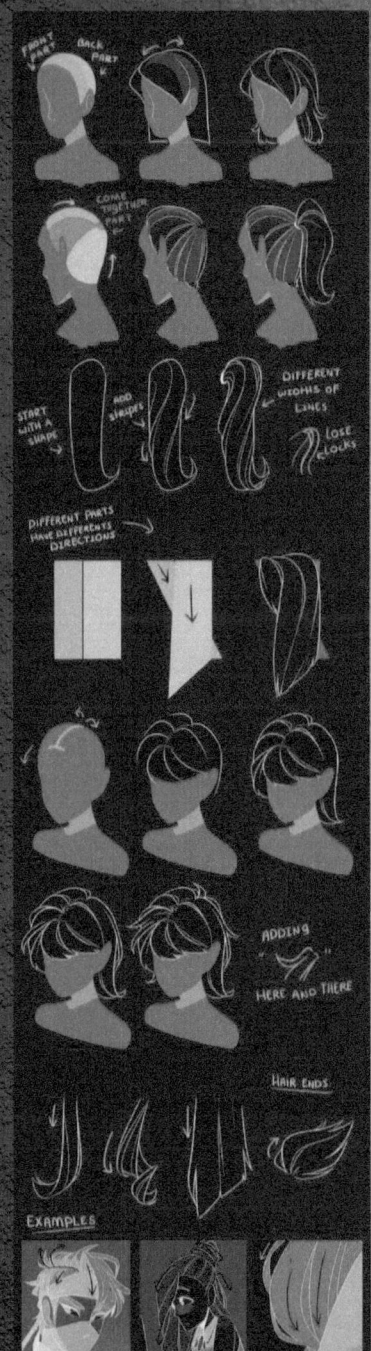
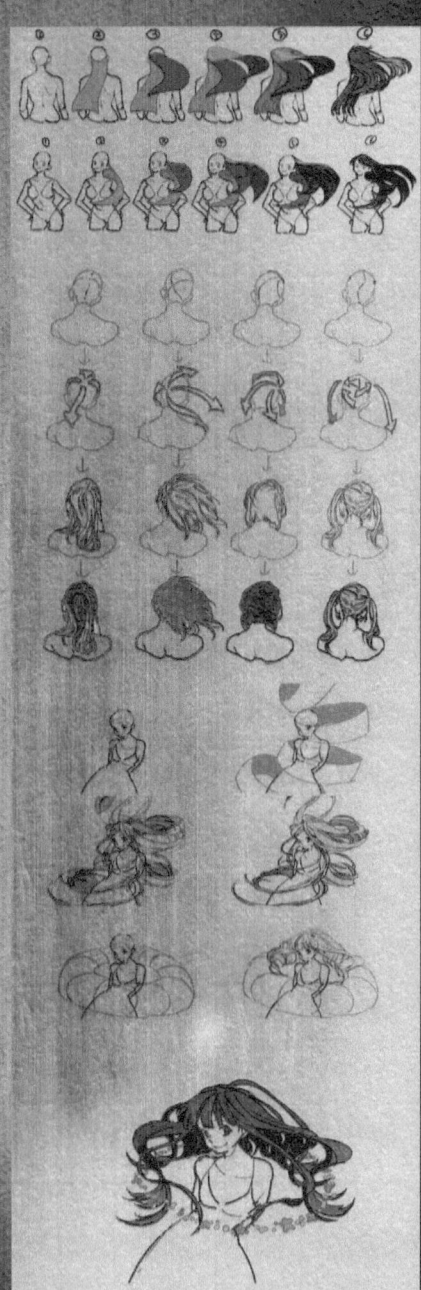

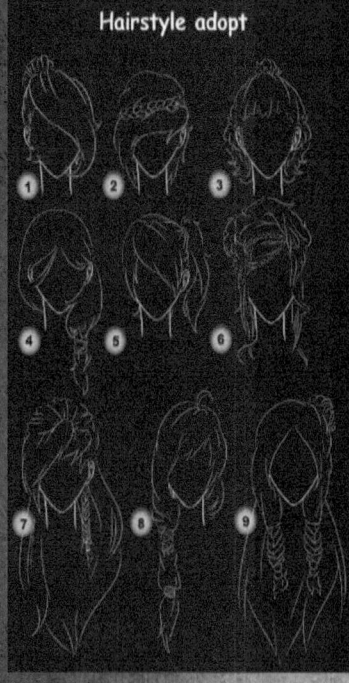
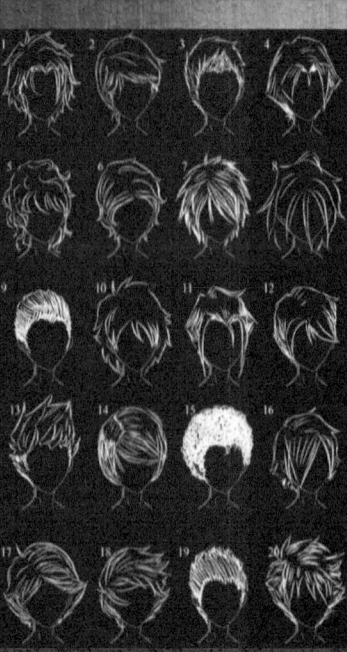
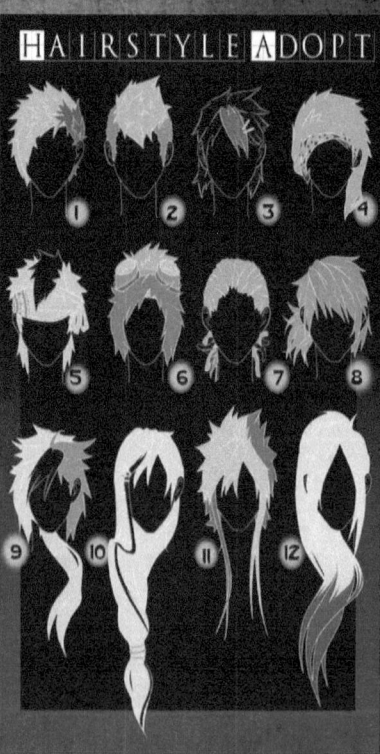

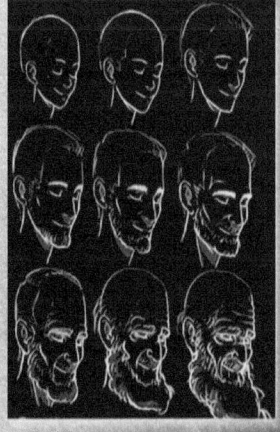
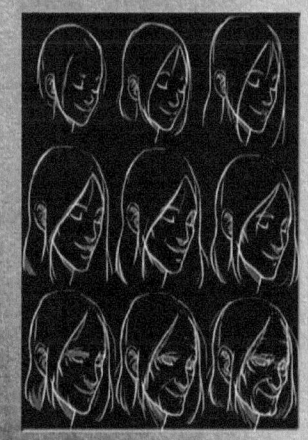
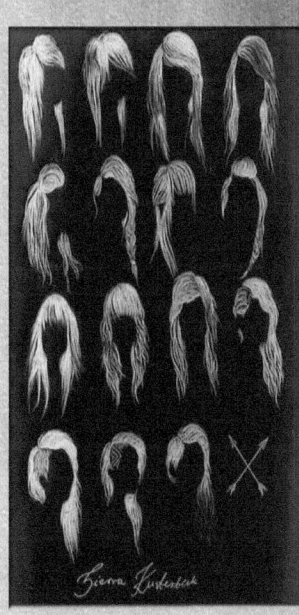
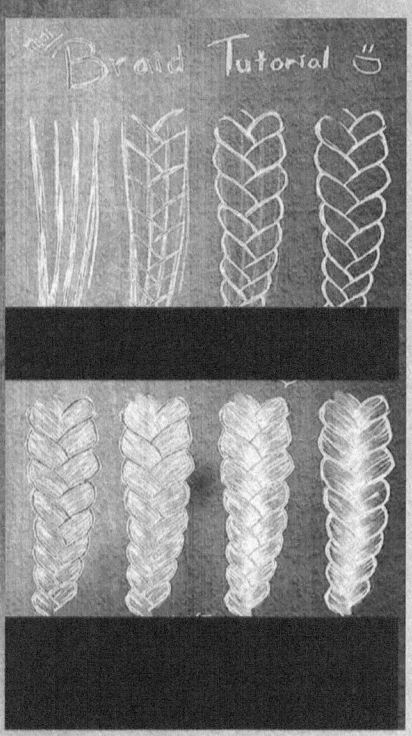

FA3

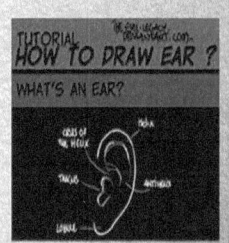
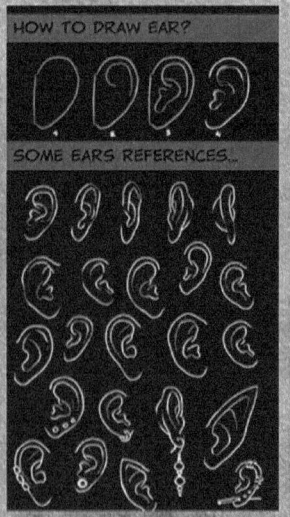
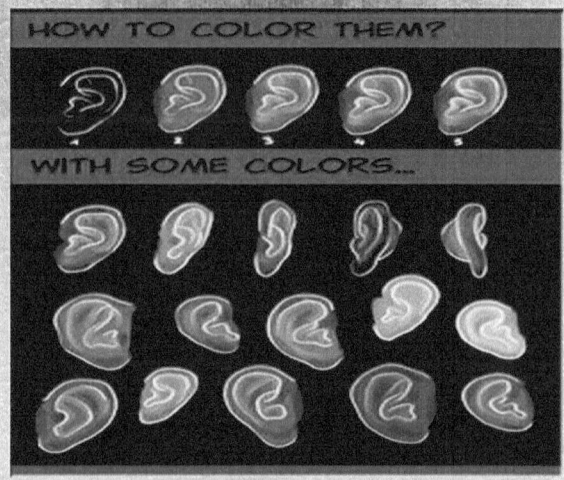

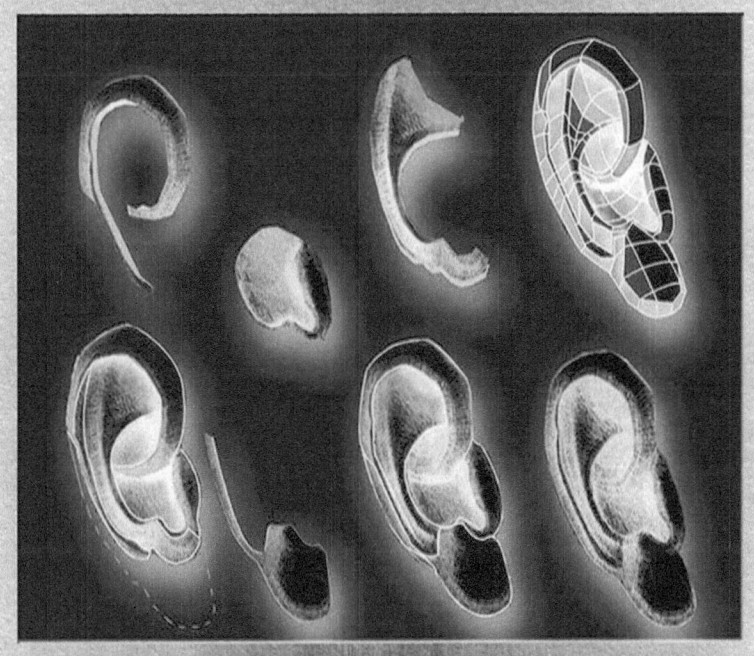
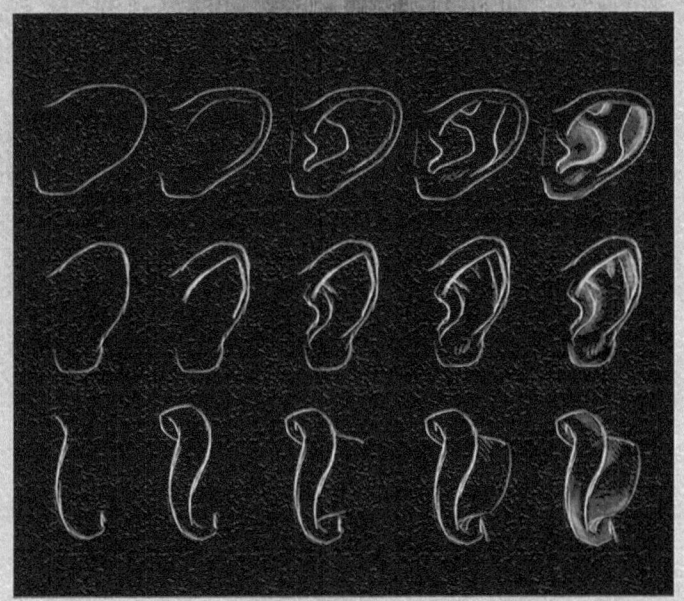

FA3

Expressions

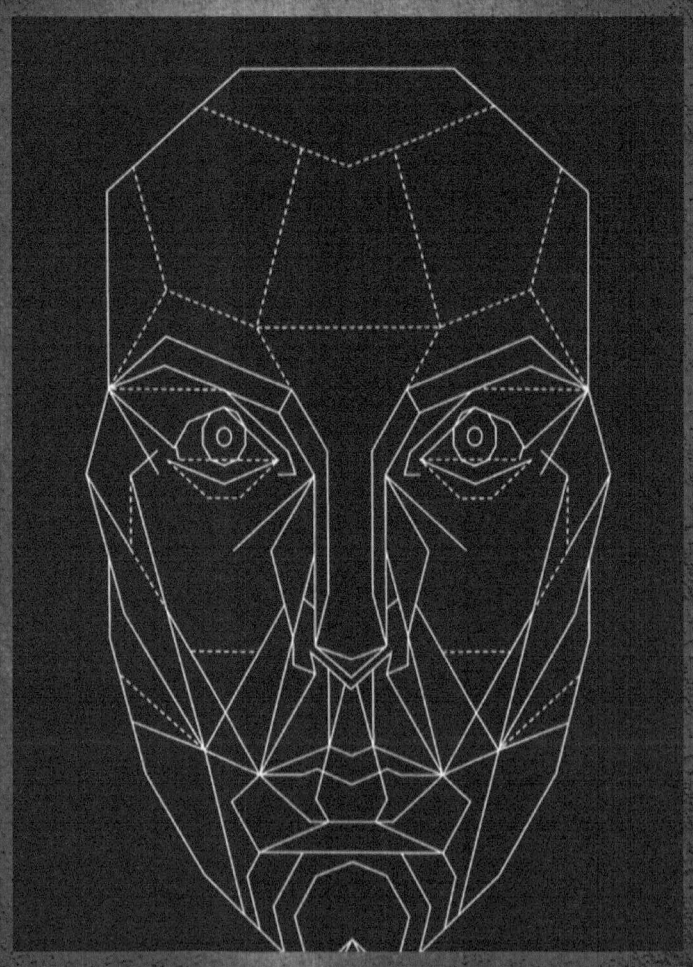

FA3

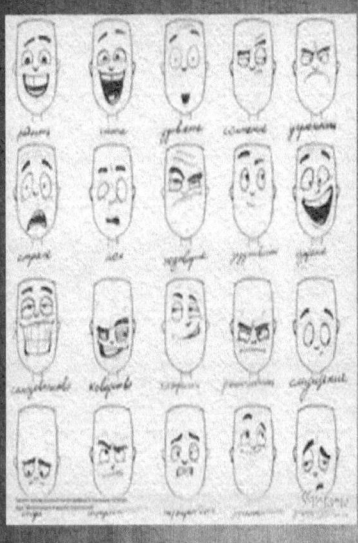
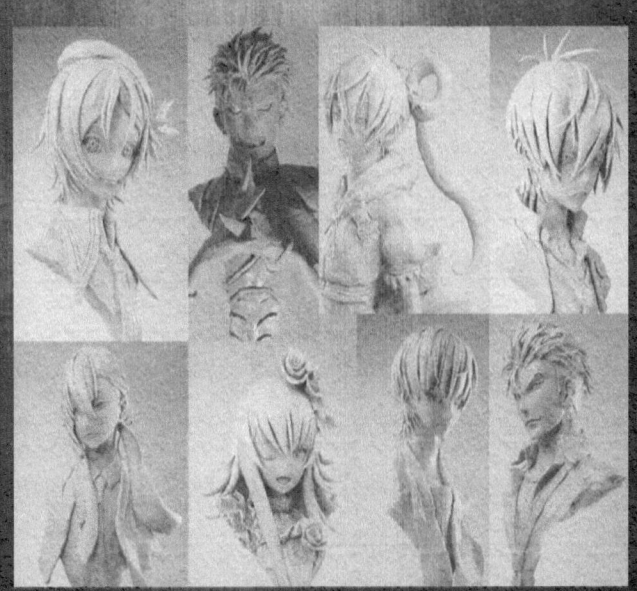

FA3

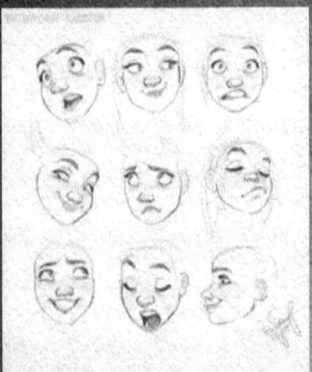
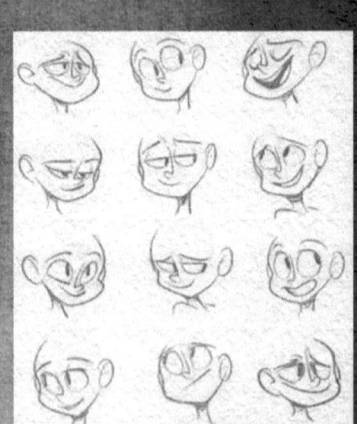
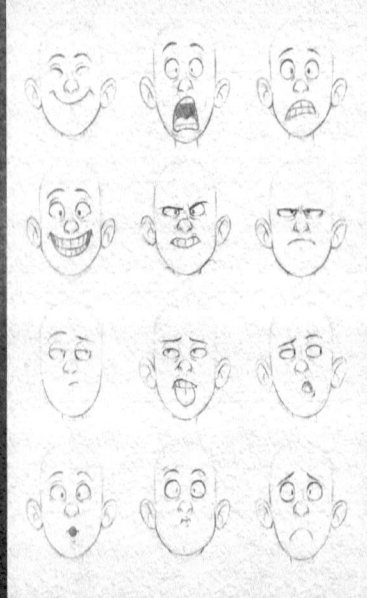

FA3

Body

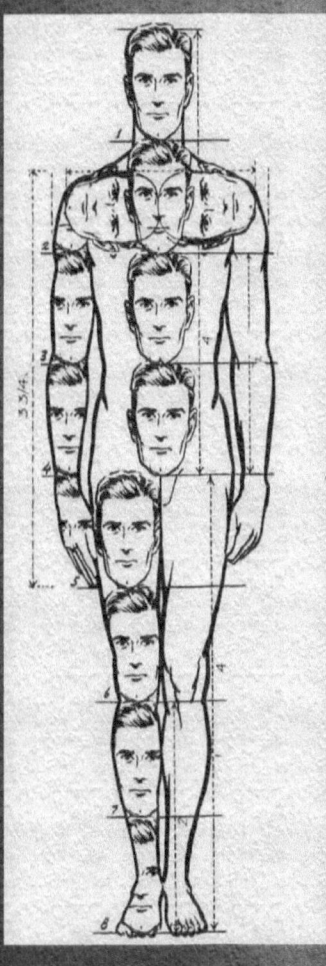

This is one of the easyest way to draw just remember eight heads will make one human body no matter what age or gender, you can always customize your charaters with set of guide lines to make more realistic art cartoon or any art.

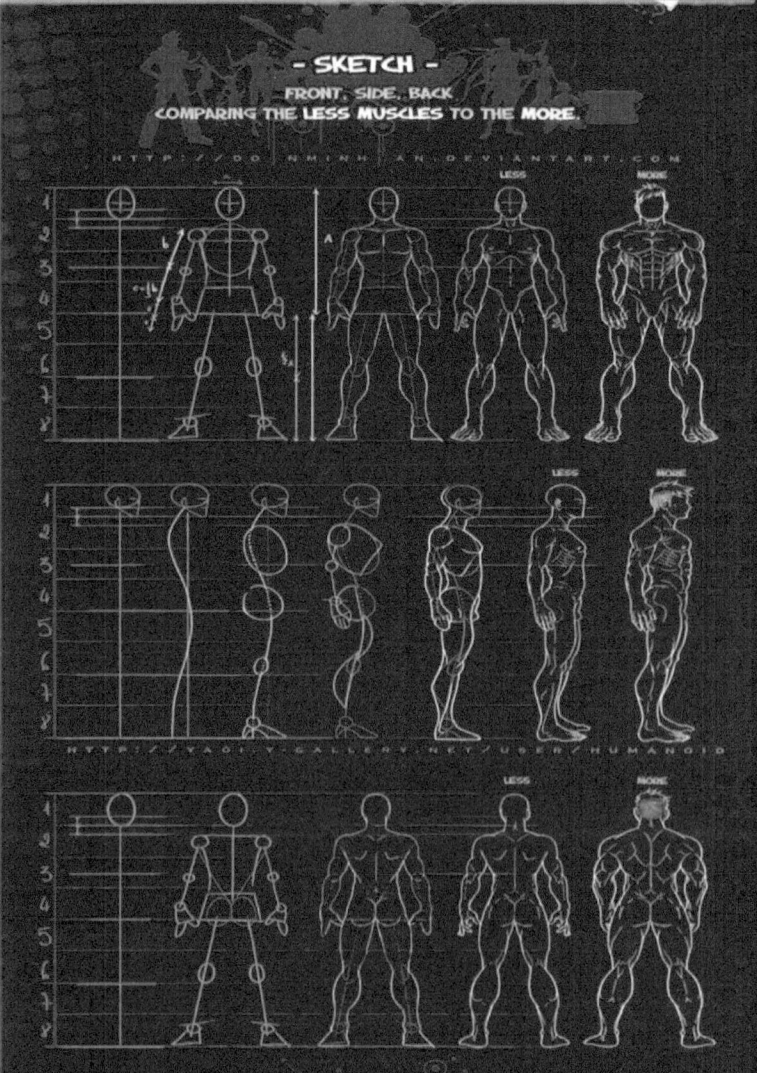

Body

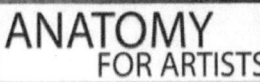

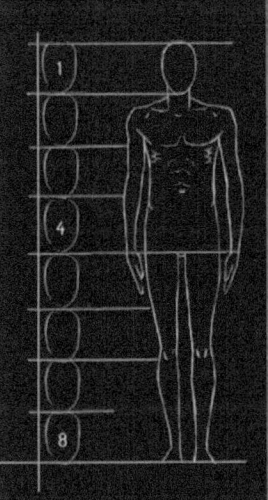

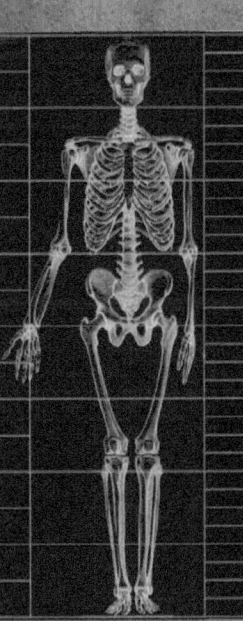

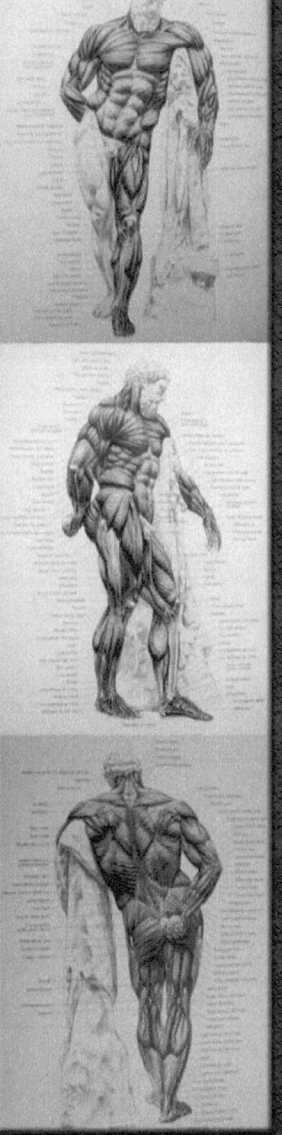

FA3

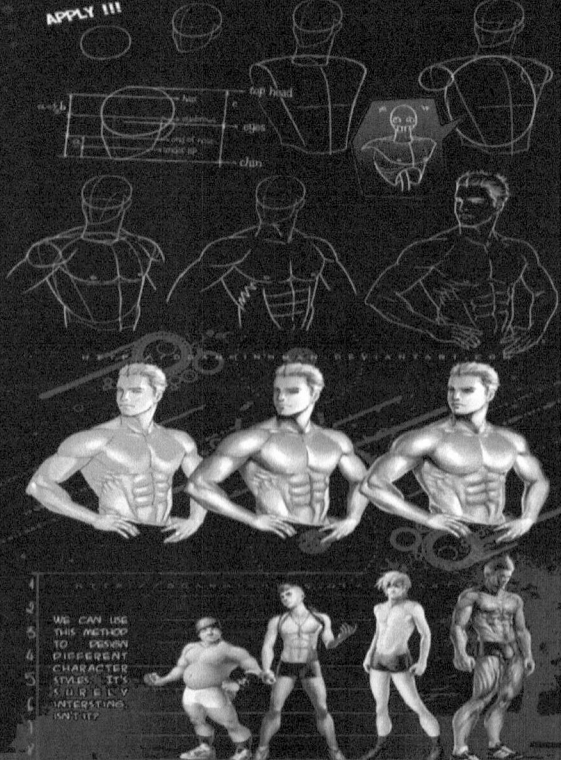

Body

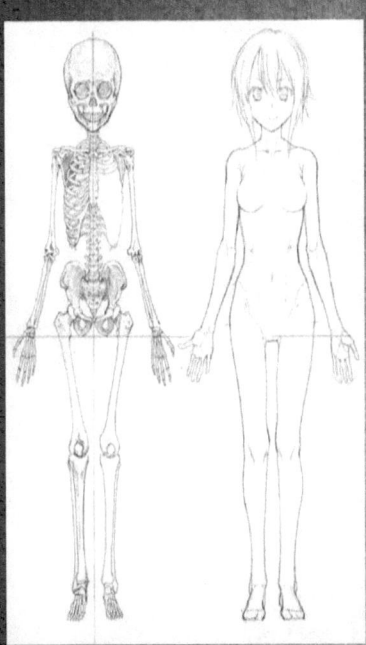
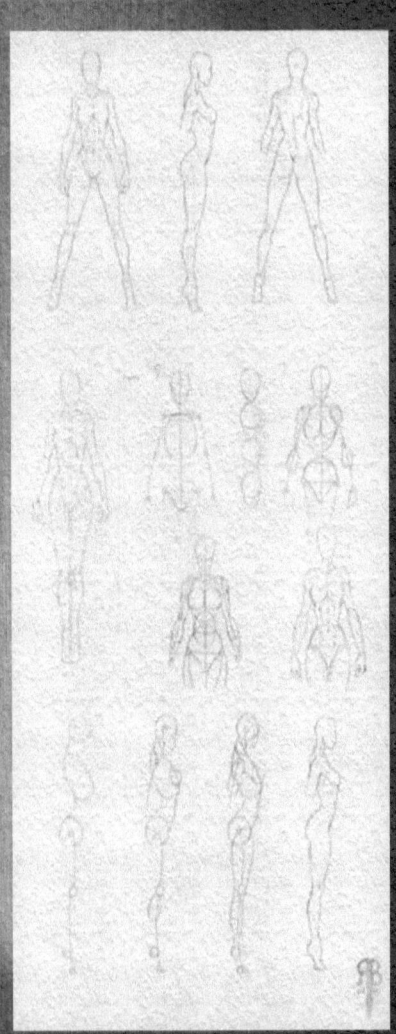

Body

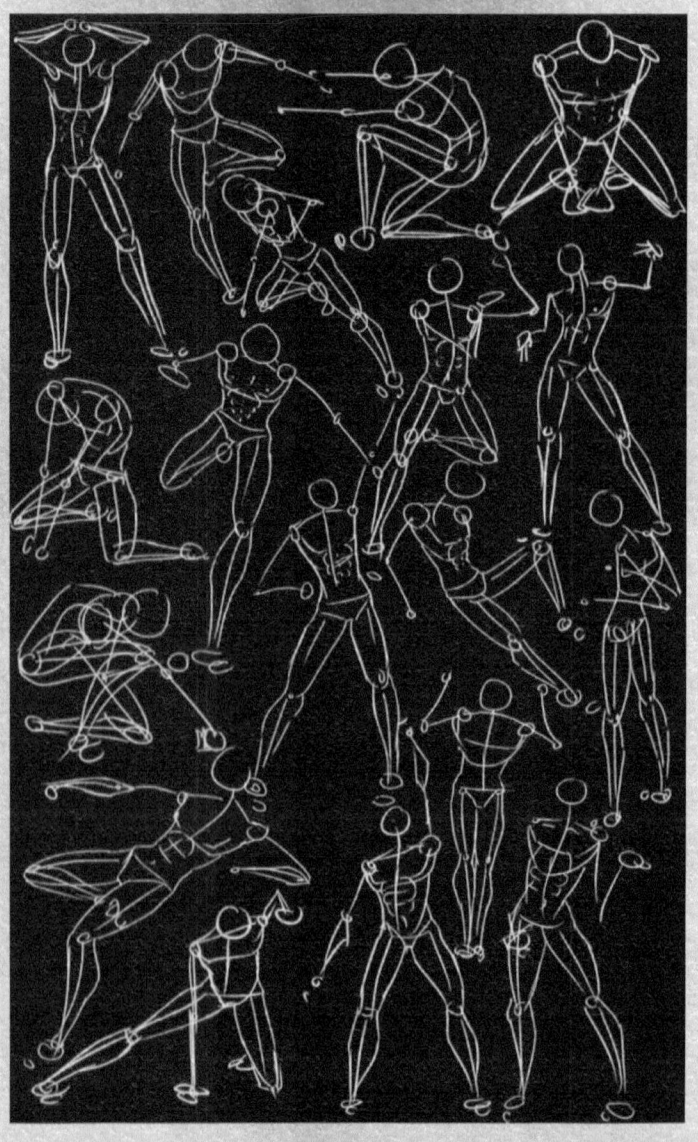

FA3

Cartoons

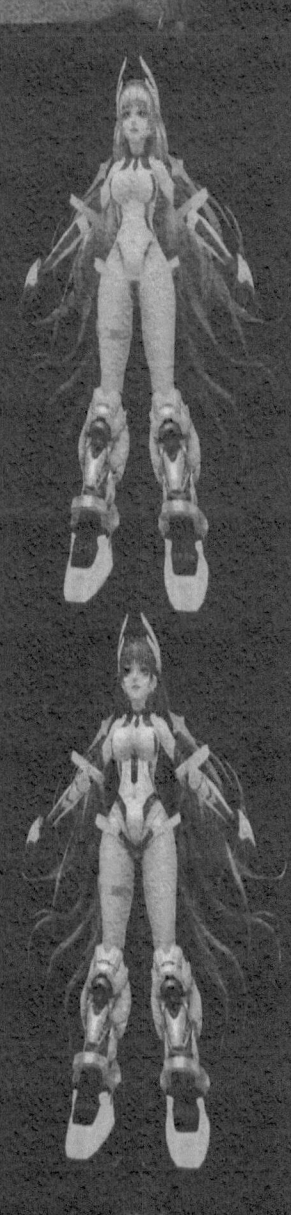

FA3

Cartoons

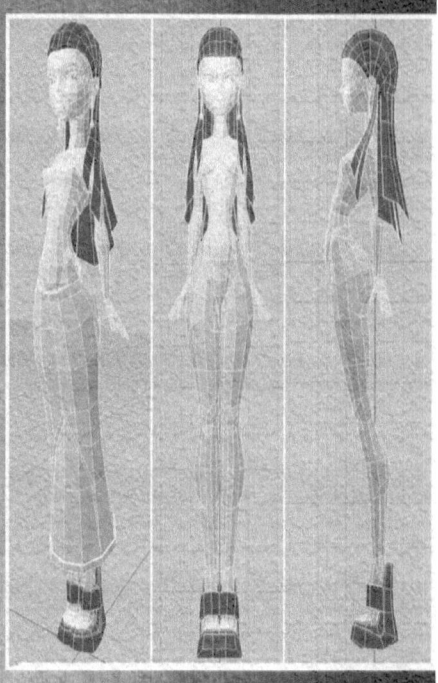

FA3

Cartoons

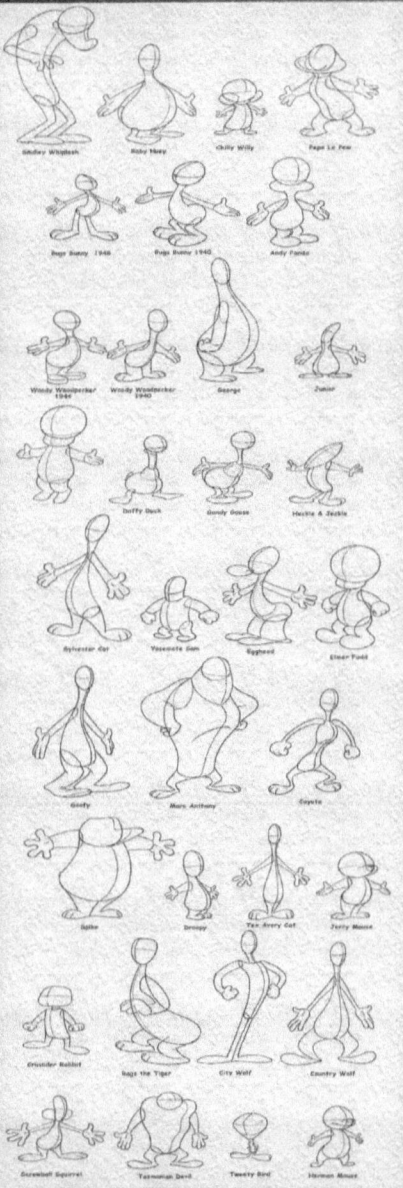
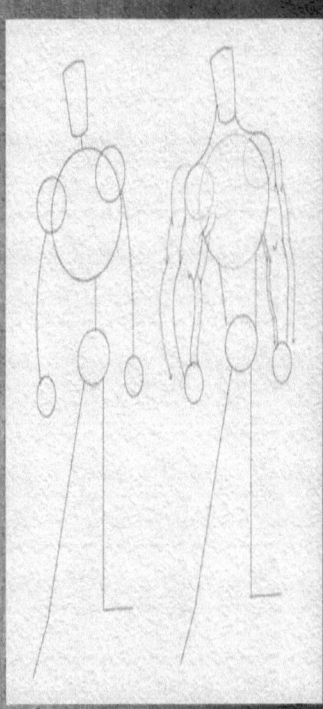

FA3

DRAWING NECK

NECK IS THICK COLLECTION OF MUSCLES IT NEEDS TO BE STRONG, KEEP THE SKULL UPRIGHT, SOME CARTOONS HAVE THIN NECK HOWEVER ITS BETTER TO HAVE UNDERSTADING ABOUT HUMAN NECK AND DRAW BETTER ACCORDING TO THE CHARACTERS

THE TWO LARGE MUSCLES IN THE NECK CAN OFTEN SEEN BULGING UNDER THE SKIN THEY TO COLLARBONE ONE ON EACH SIDE

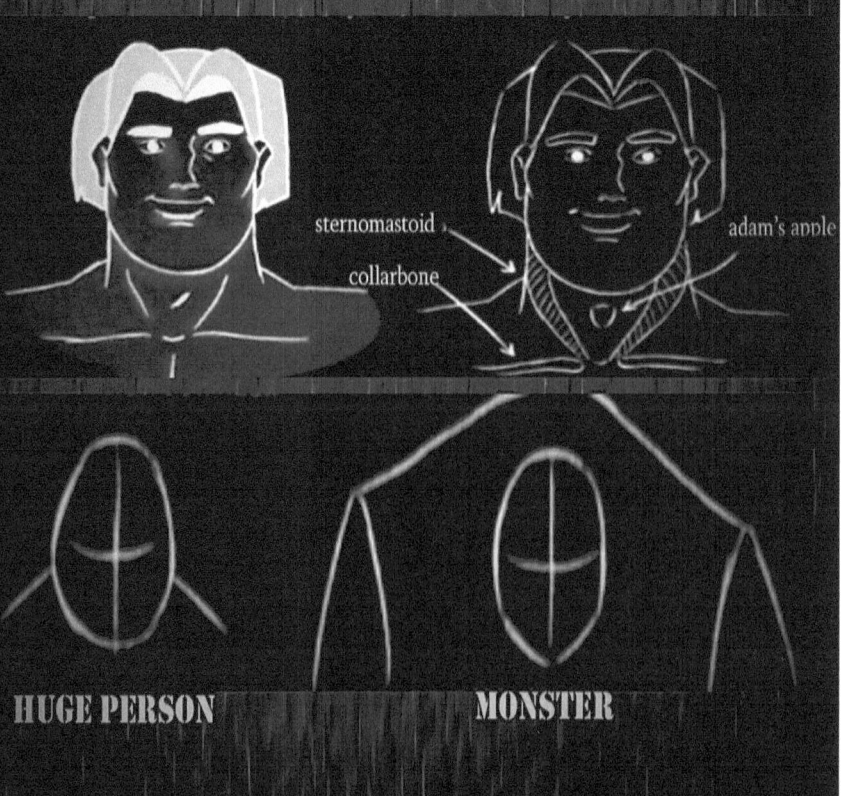

HUGE PERSON   **MONSTER**

DRAWING HANDS

MOST OF THE FAMOUS CARTOONS HAVE 4 FINGERS LIKE IN DISNEY SOME HAVE 3 HOWEVER YOU CAN EXPERIMENT WITH YOUR CHOICE 3,6,9 HOW MANY EVR YOU LIKE

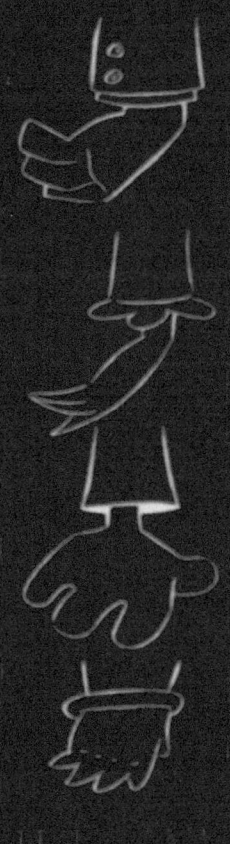

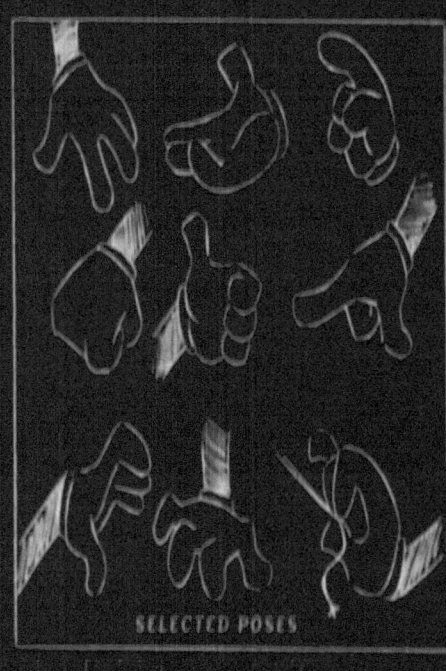

SELECTED POSES

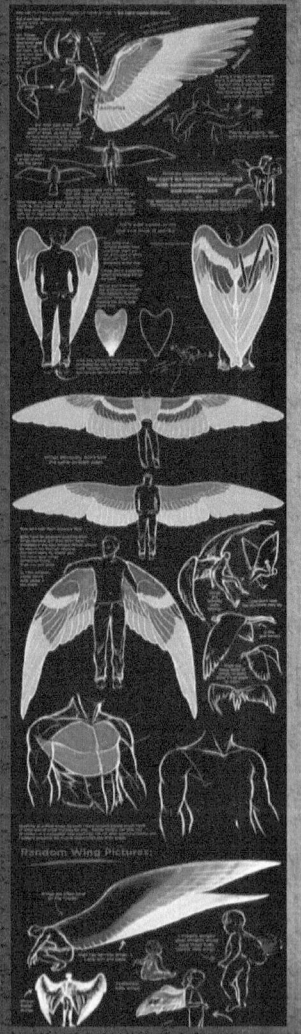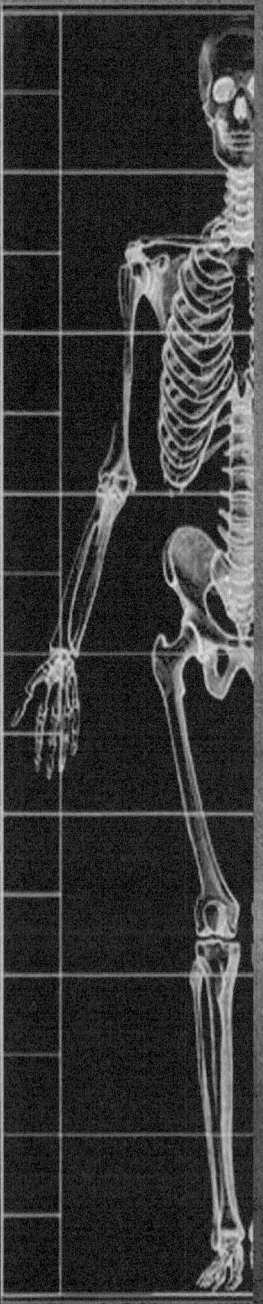

Thats the exact lengh the hand should be for all ages and gender

FA3

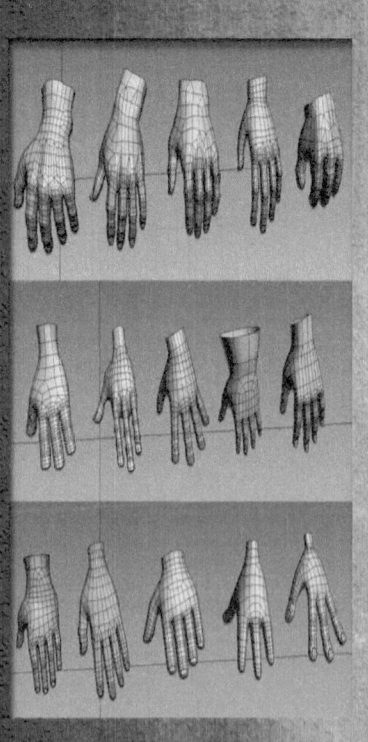
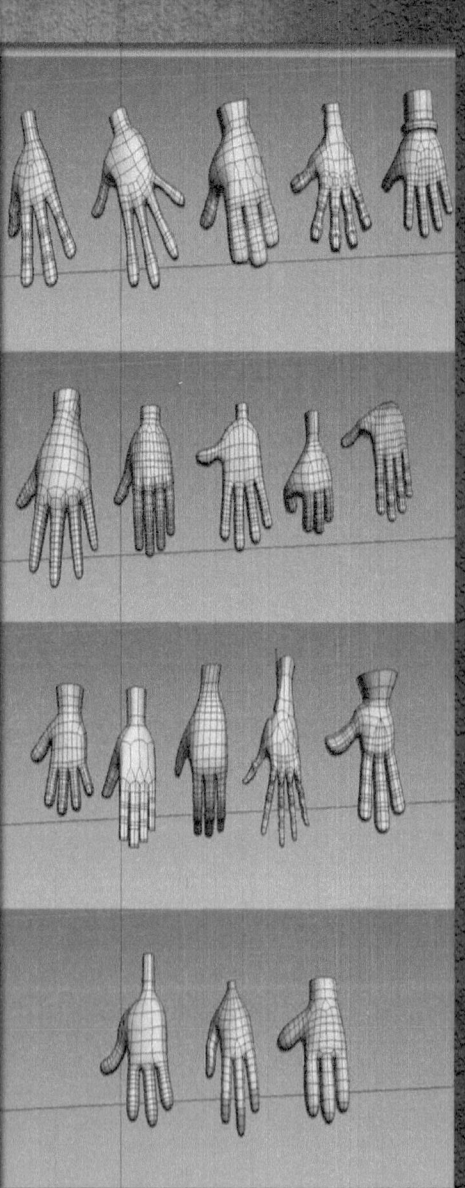

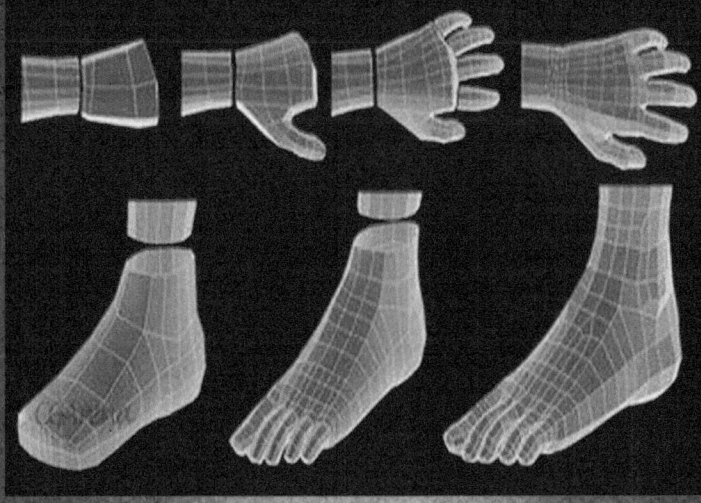
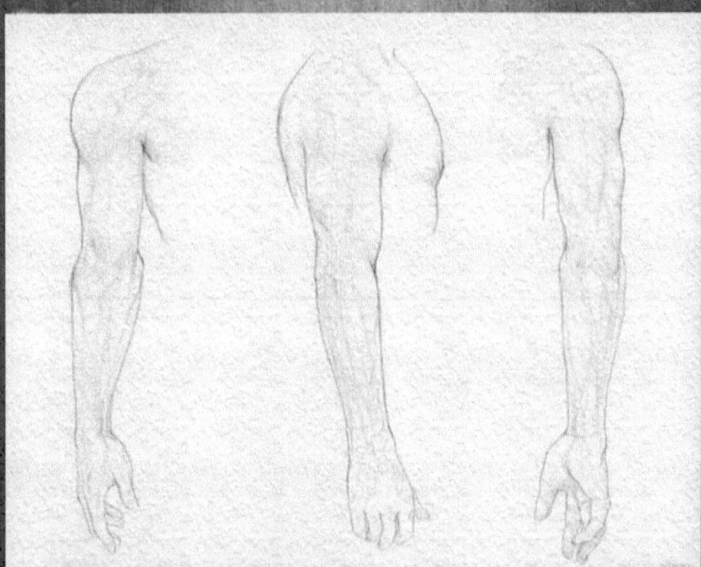

FA3

TUTORIAL
HOW TO DRAW FEET?

WHAT'S A FEET?

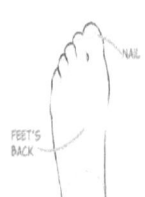
BACK

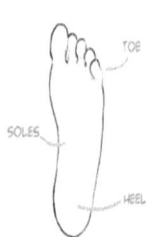
FACE

HOW TO DRAW FEET

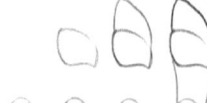
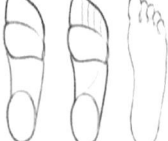
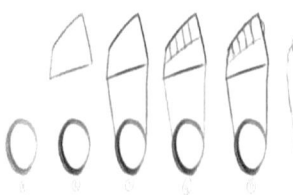
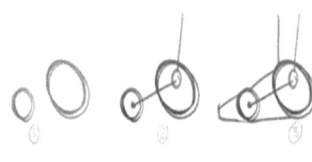
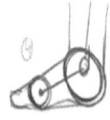
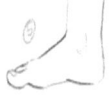

SOME FEET REFERENCES...

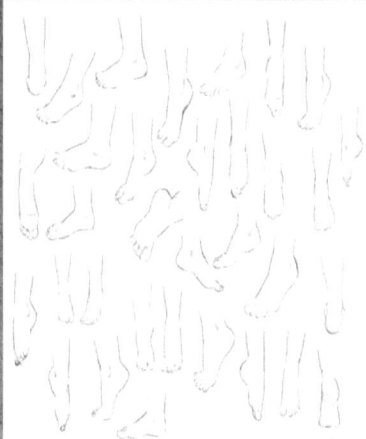

AND IN COLOR...

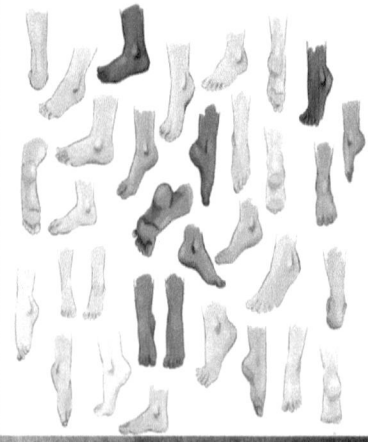

FA3

Posture

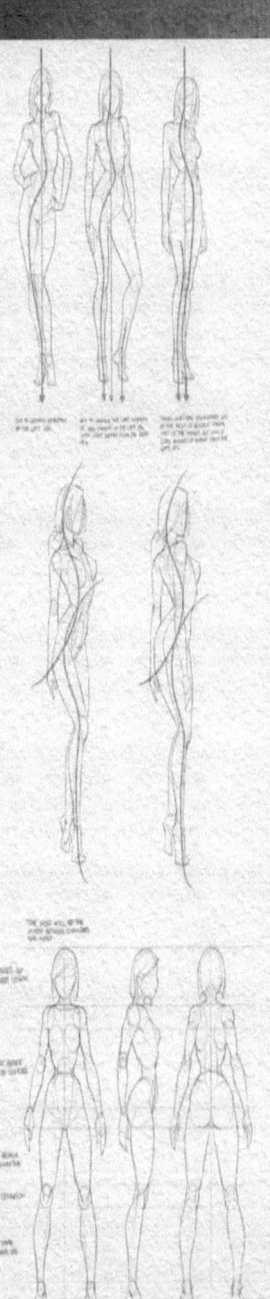
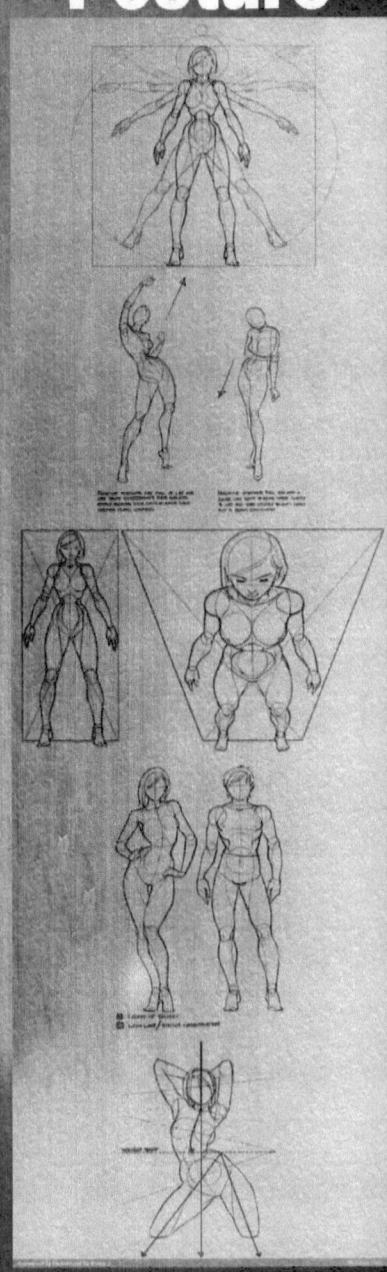

FA3

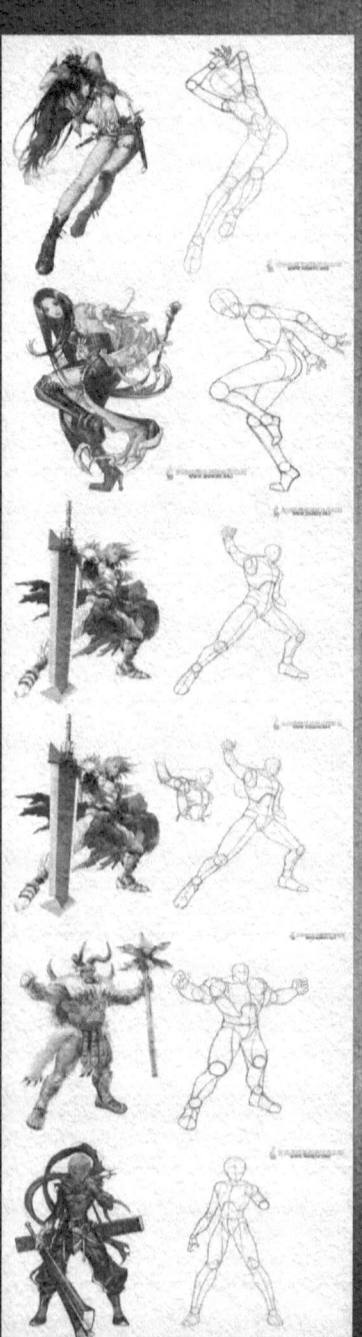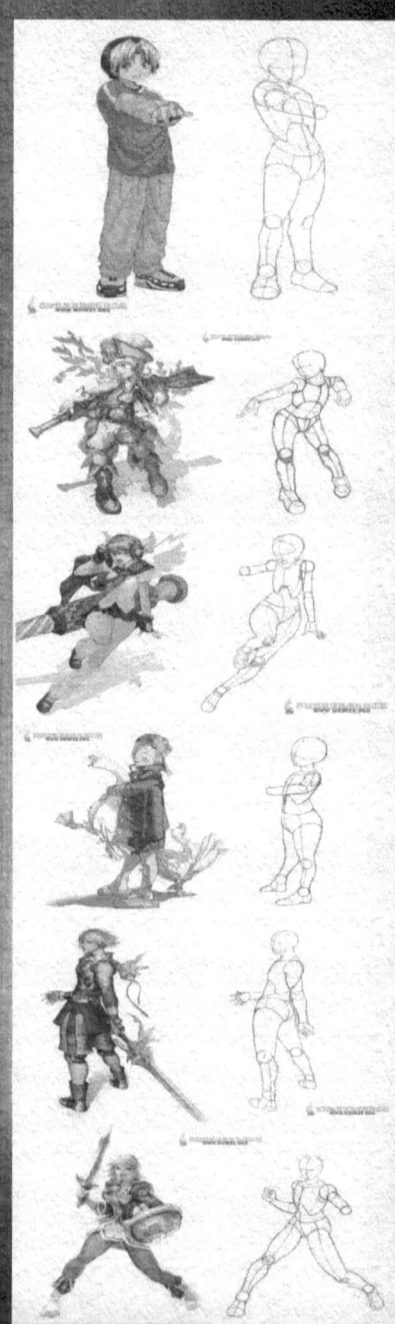

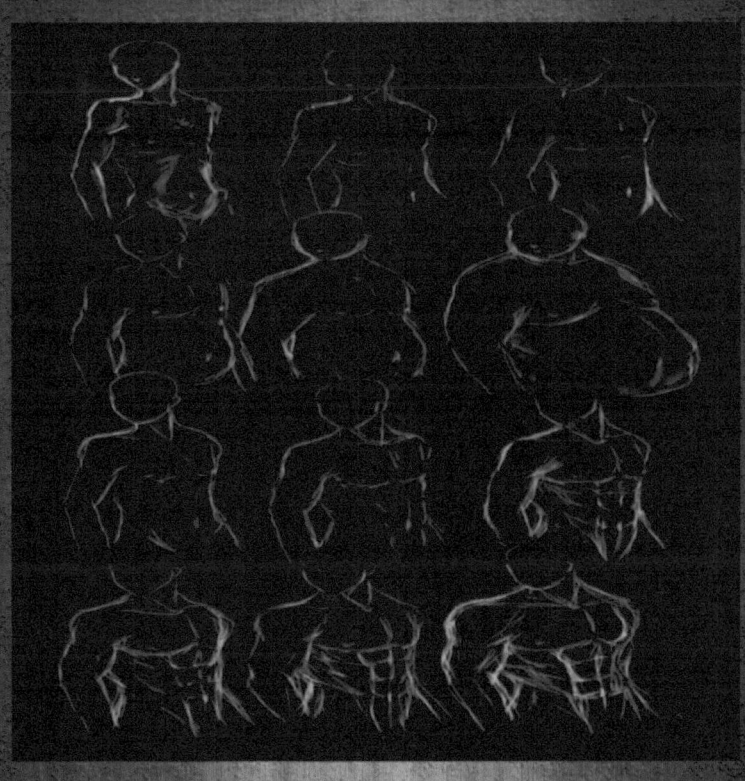
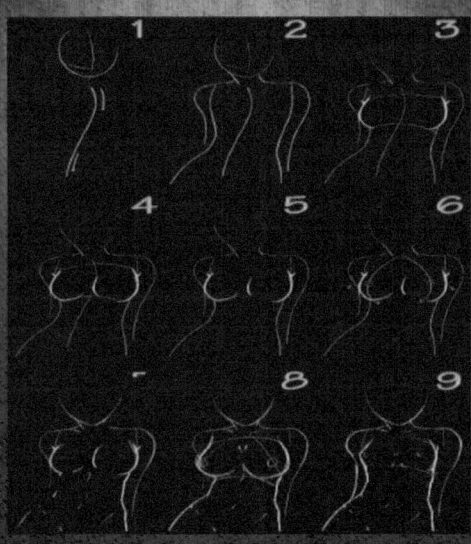

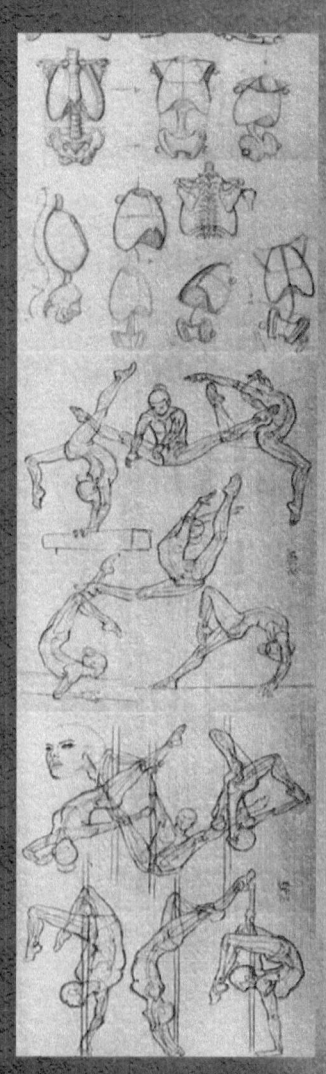
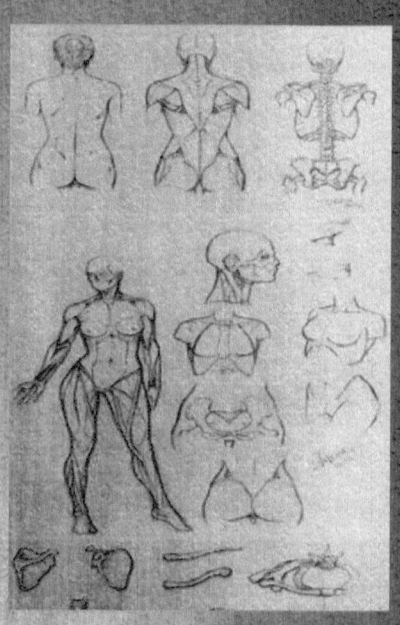

FA3

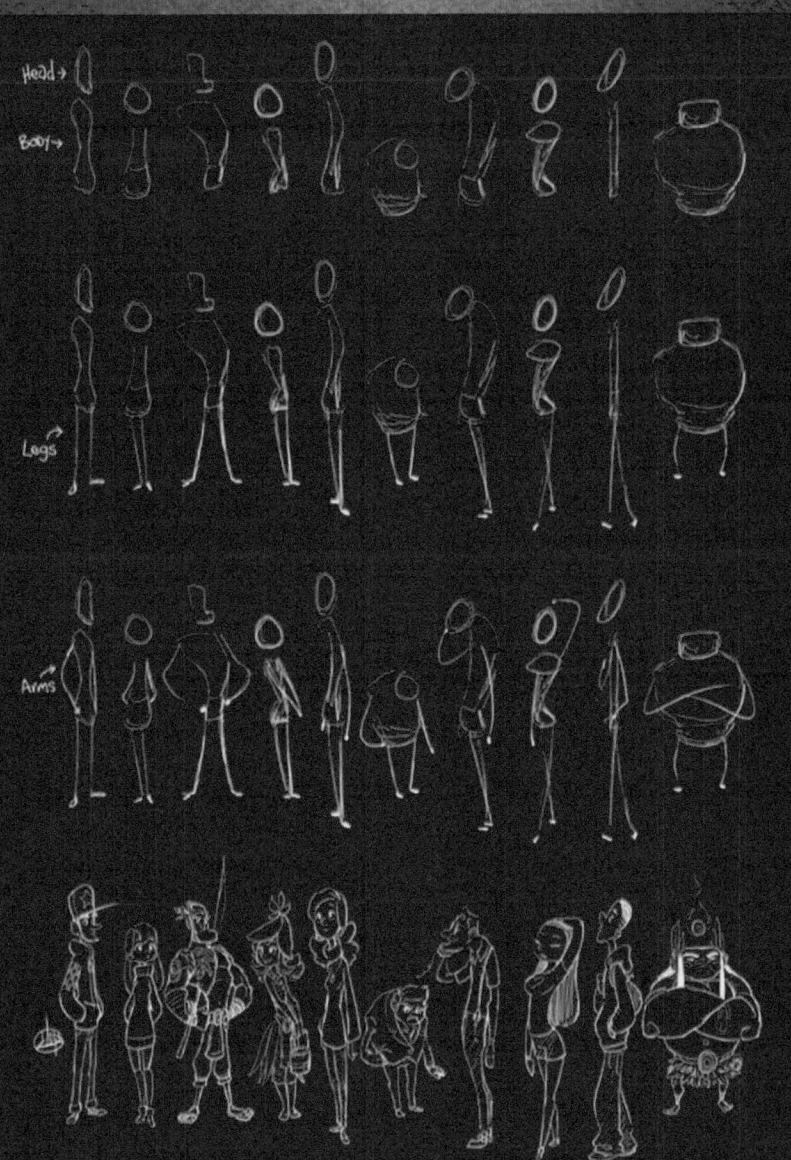

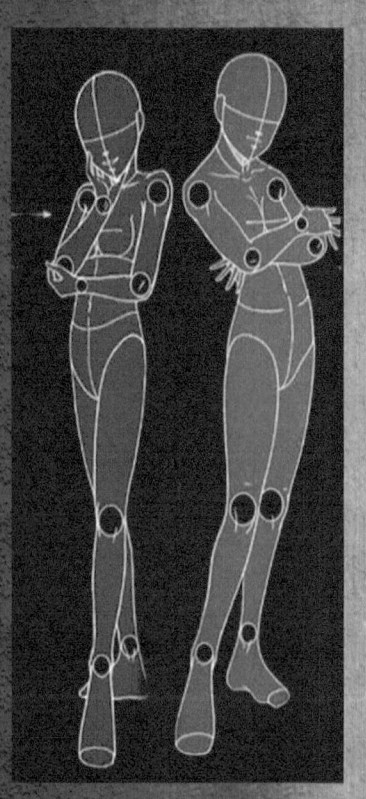
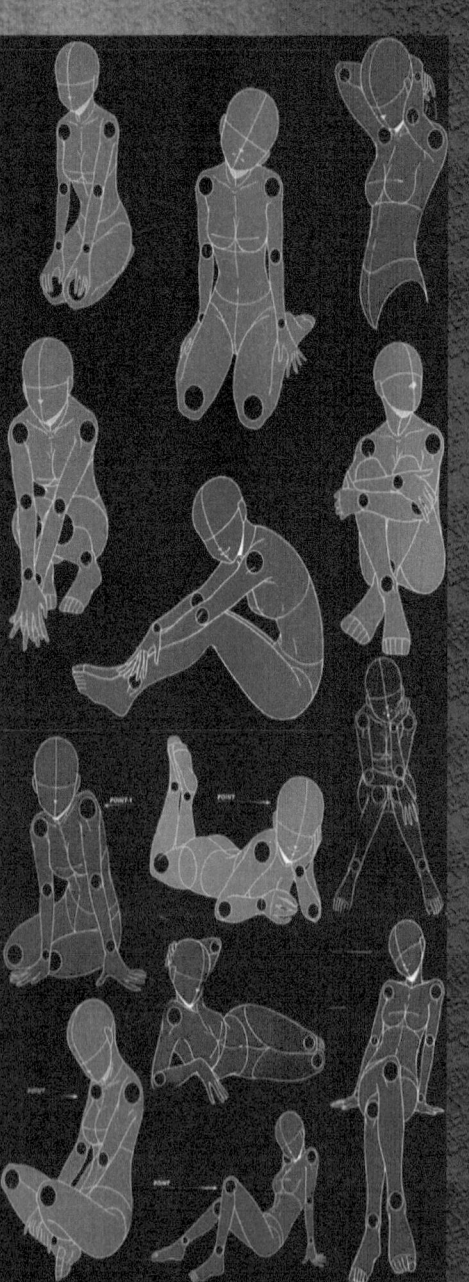

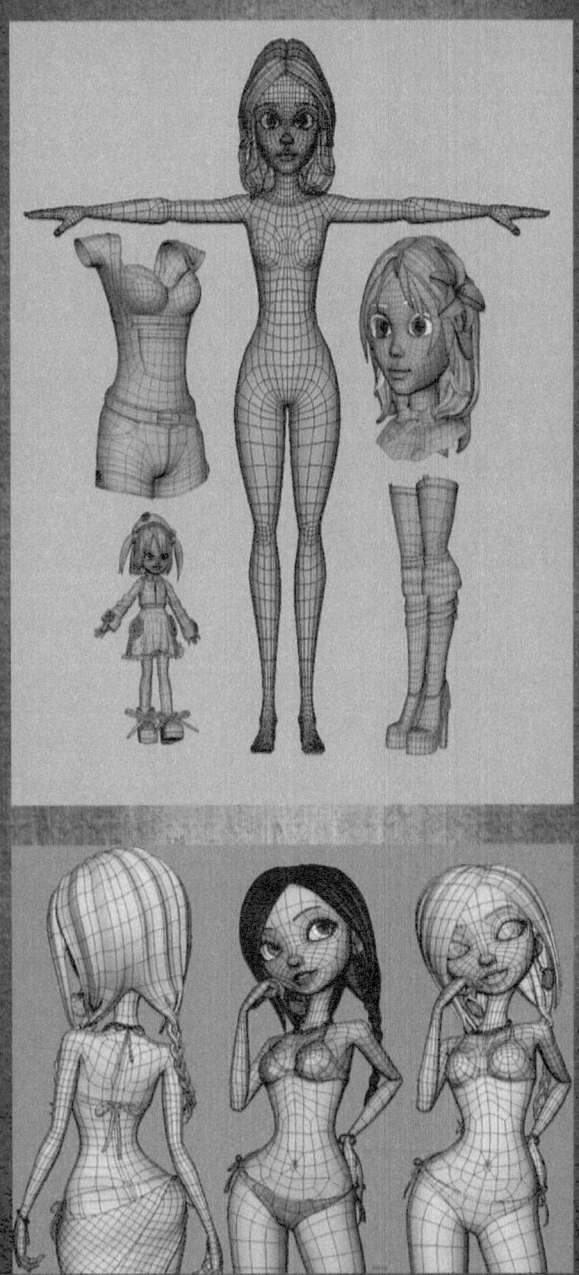

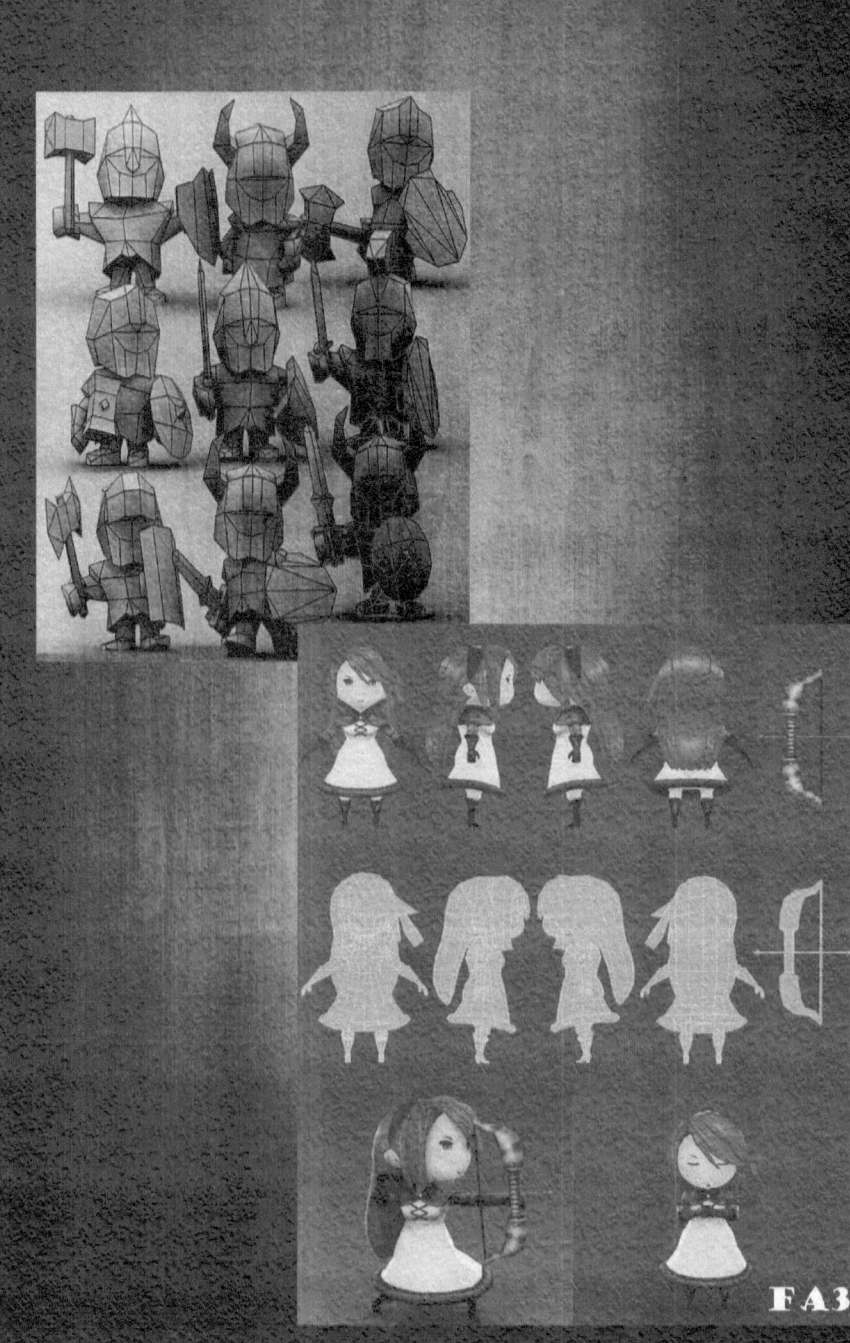

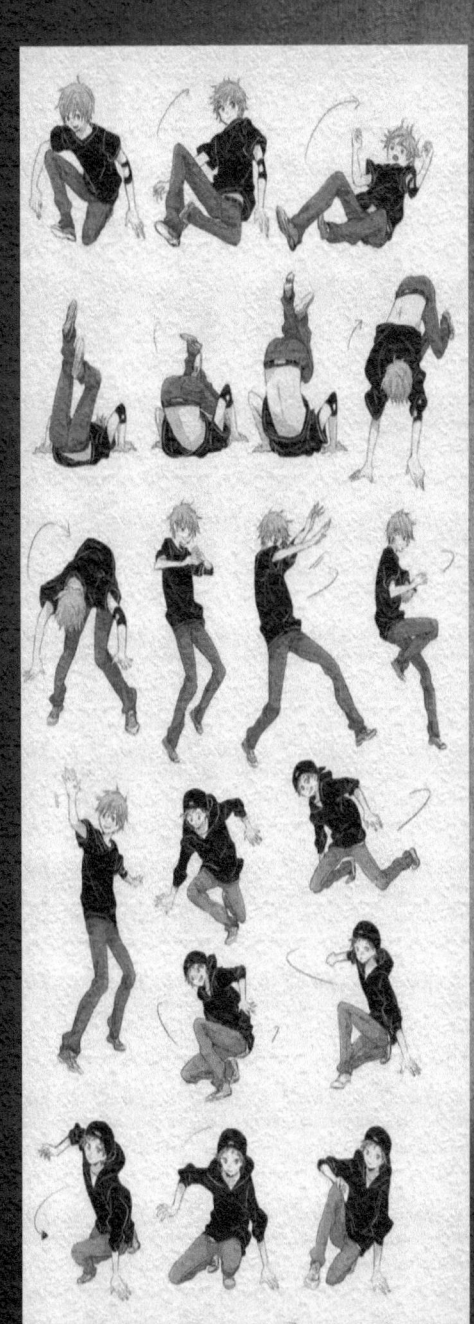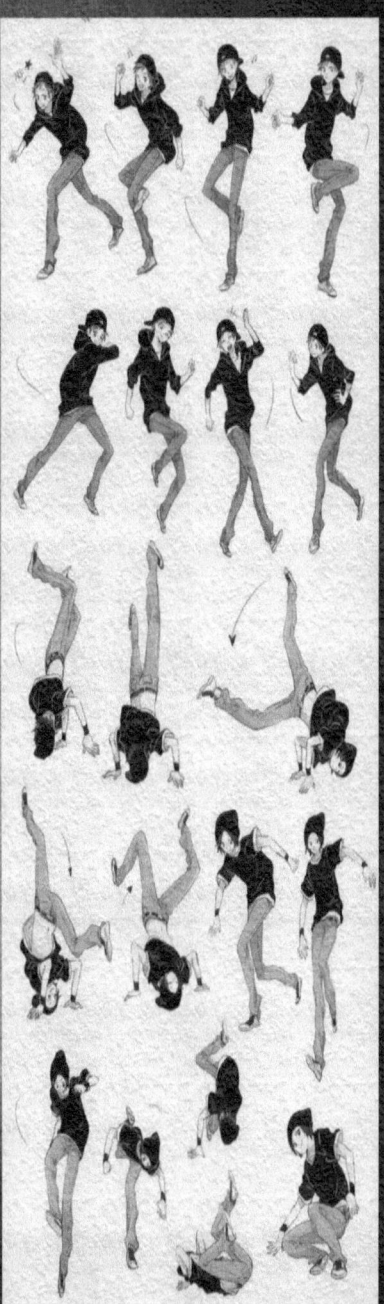

FA3

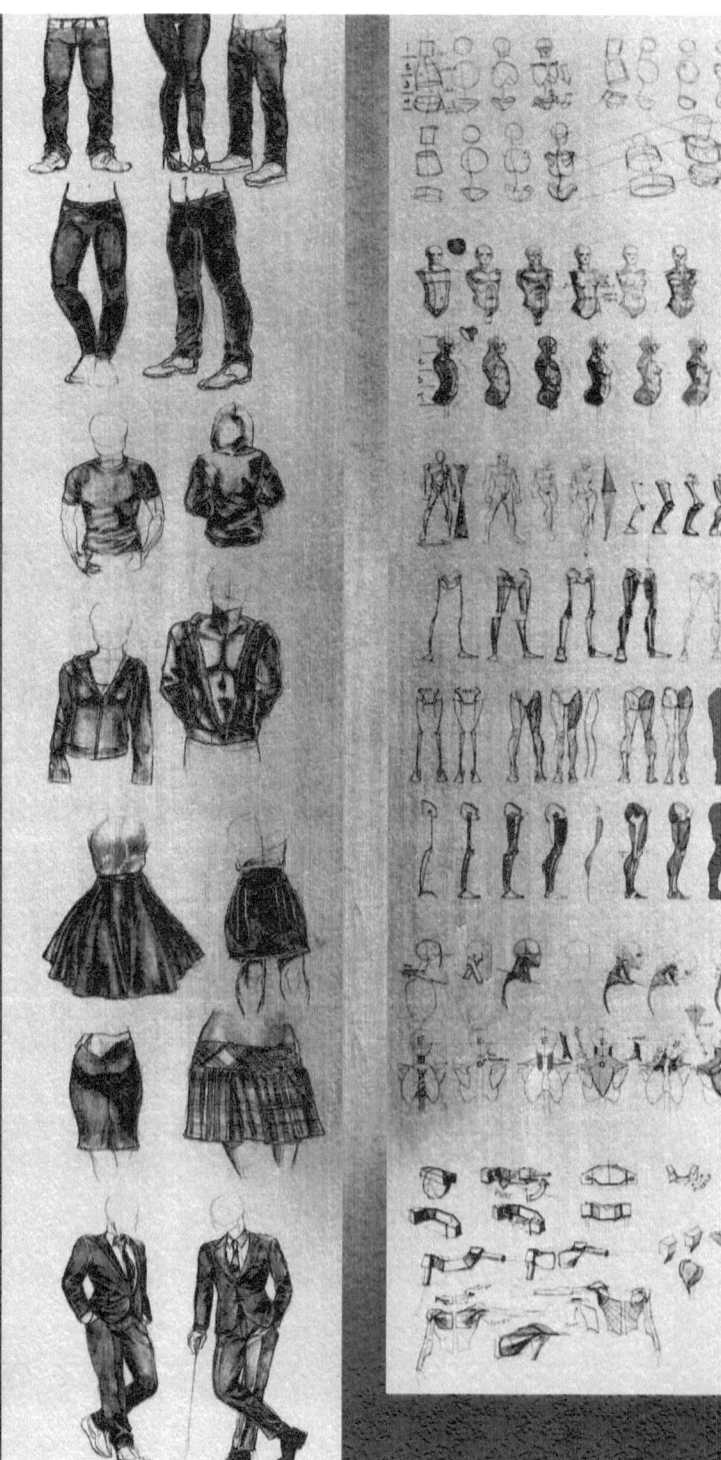

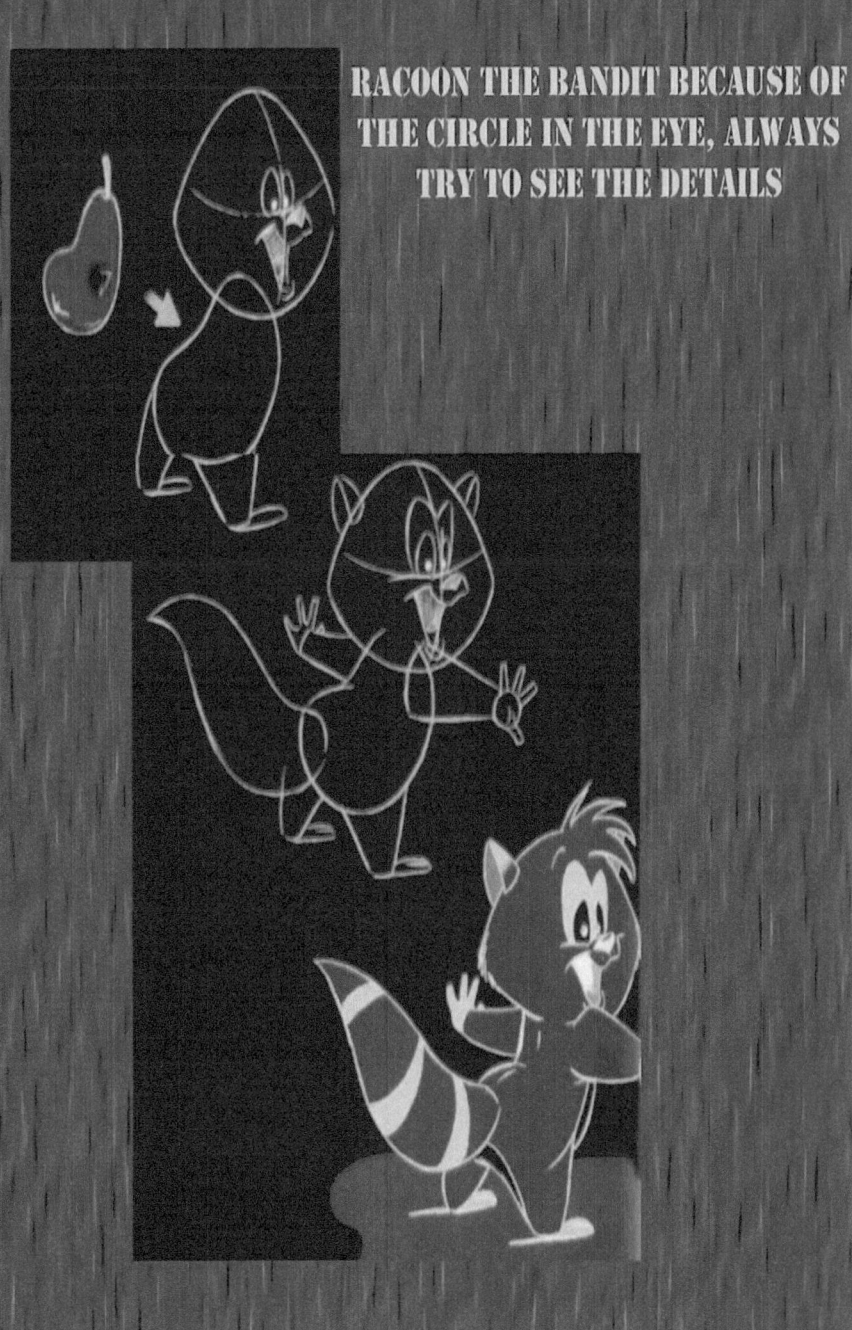

MOST OF THE CARTOON CHARACTERS ARE NOTORIOUS, THE MOTION SHOULD MATCH THE ACTION

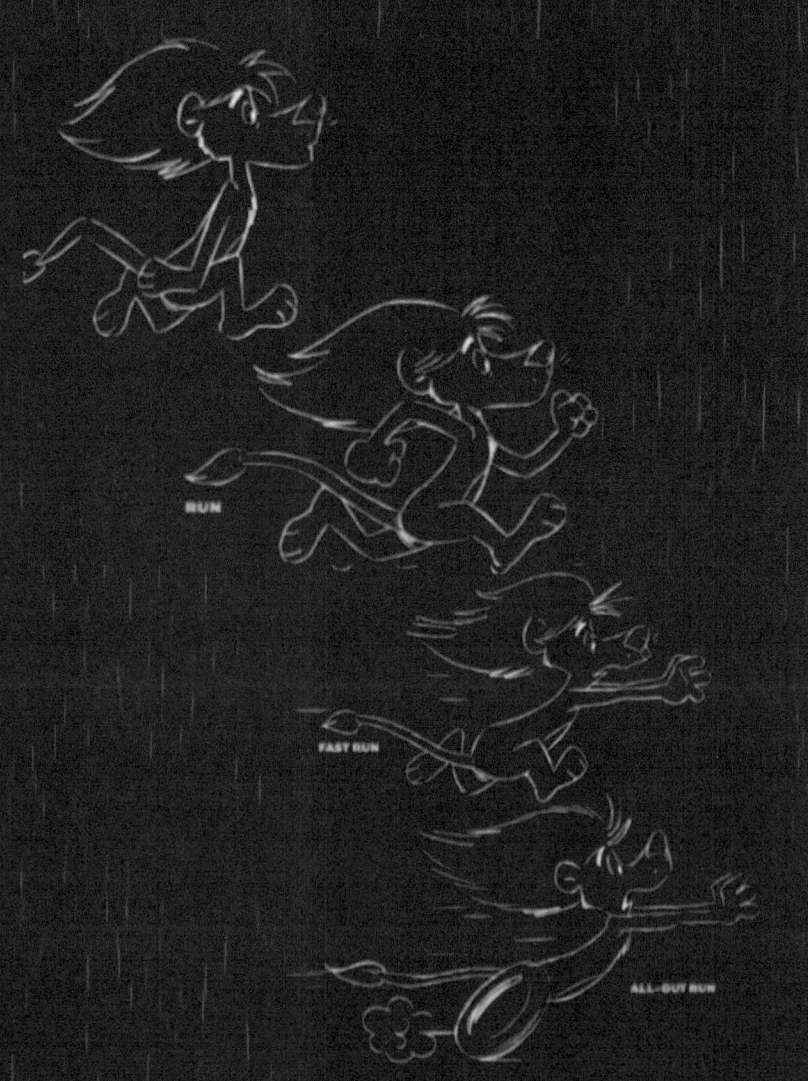

DRAWING SIDE AND BACK VIEW

NOTICE CAREFULLY YOU'LL SEE THE UPPER BODY DOESN'T STAND STRAIGHT UP INSTEAD IT IS PULLED IN THE DIRECTION OF THE HEAD AND NECK, WHICH HANGS SLIGHTLY FORWARD.

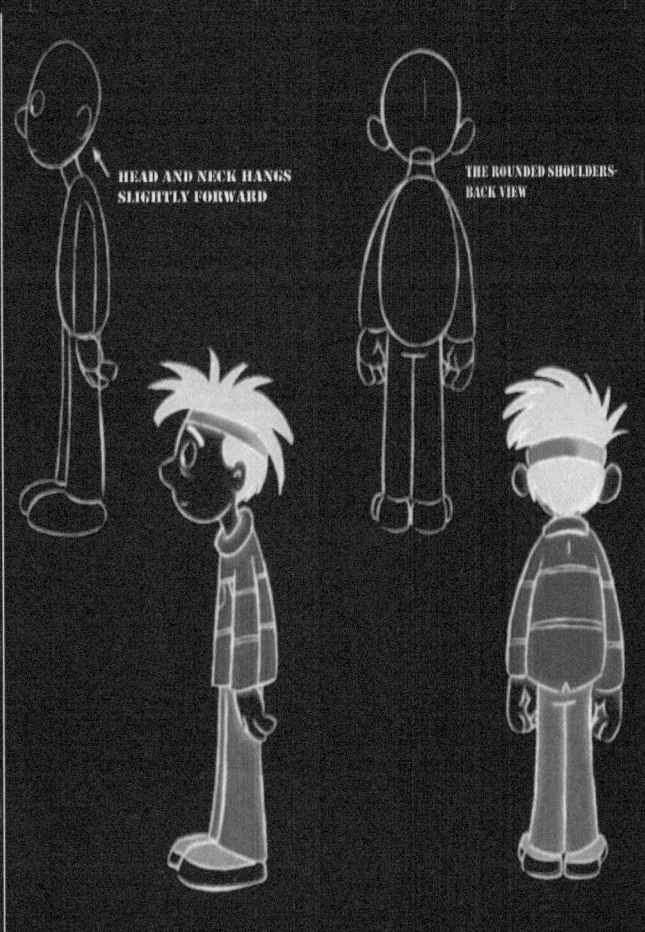

HEAD AND NECK HANGS SLIGHTLY FORWARD

THE ROUNDED SHOULDERS- BACK VIEW

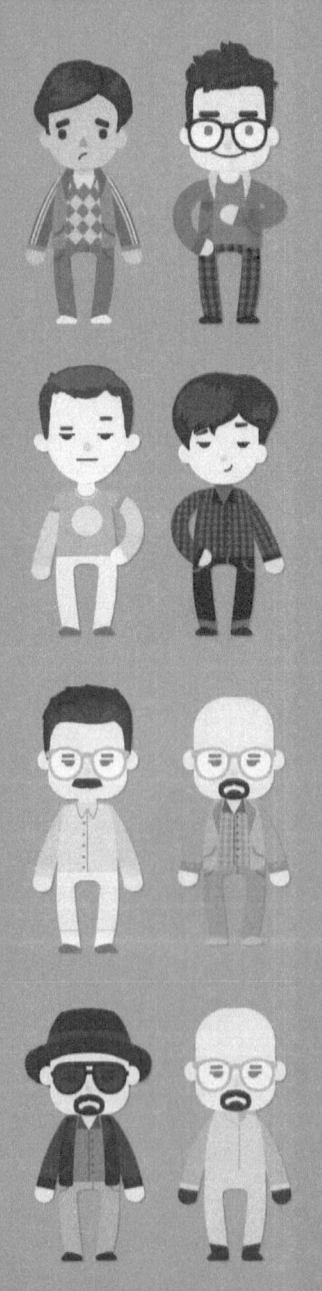
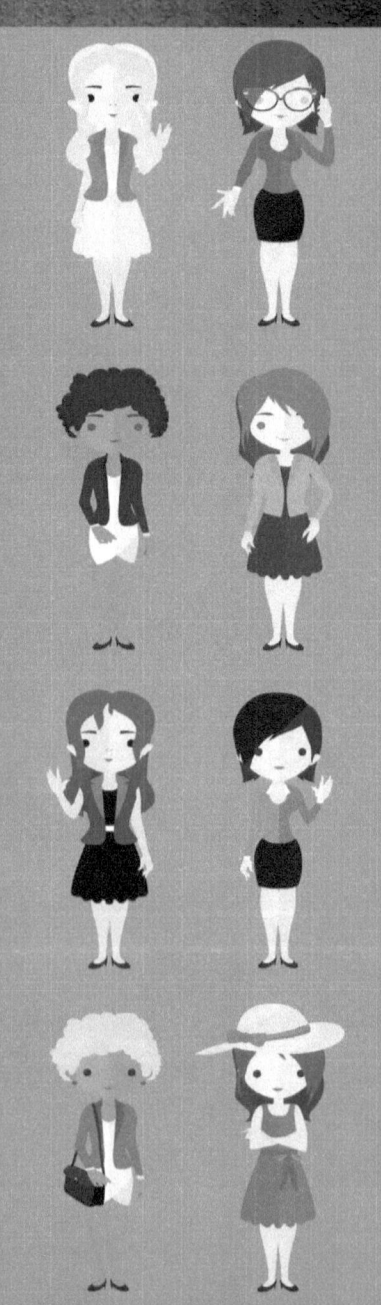

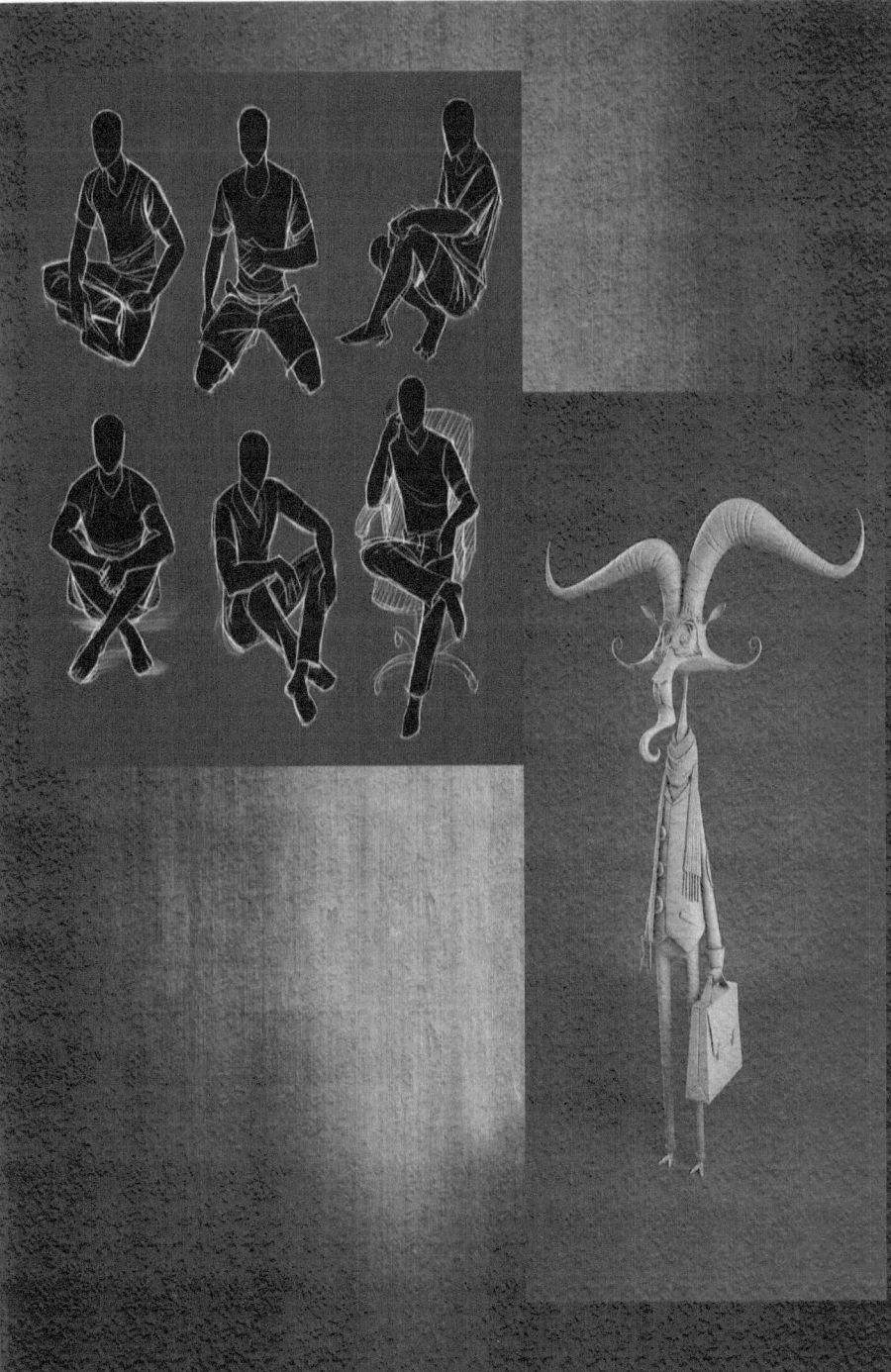

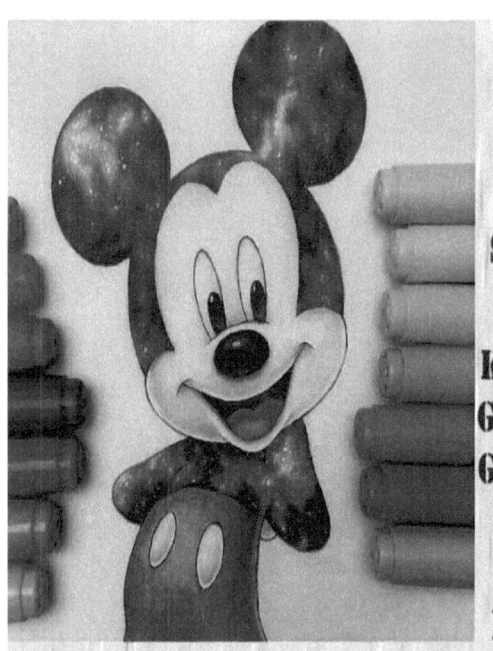

ONCE YOU GET USED TO THE OUTLINE AND BASIC SHAPES START COLORING

KEEP PRACTICING TILL YOU GET IT RIGHT AND YOU WILL GET IT RIGHT, DONT WORRY ABOUT HOW LONG IT WIL TAKE LET IT TAKE DAYS, MONTHS OR YEARS . KEEP PRATICING YOU WILL ACHIVE LIKE PASTEL.ETTE

NEXT CHAPTER WILL BE BASICS ABOUT PERSPECTIVES

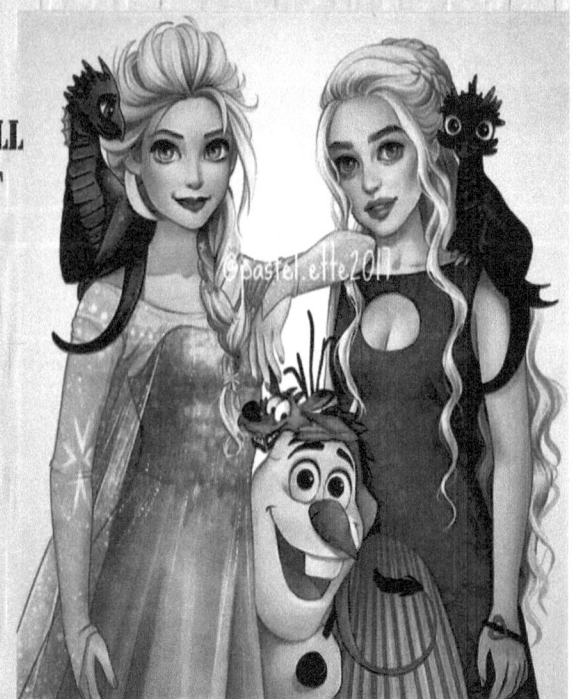

Chapter 2
Basic Perspectives

WITHOUT UNDERSTANDING PERSPECTIVE WE CANT CREATE STORY AND WORLD AROUND US

IN THIS BOOK THIER ARE COLLECTION OF MASTER ARTIST, AROUND THE GLOBE AND THIER TEACHINGS ITS BEST TECHNIQUES I HAVE FELLOWED. PRACTICE AS MUCH AS POSSIBLE DAILY TILL IT BECOMES MUSCLE MEMORY

ONE POINT PERSPECTIVE

SINCES NOT ALL THE OBJECTS HAVE PARALLEL SIDES OR ANY SIDES AT ALL, YOU MAY FIND IT HELPFULL TO THINK WHATEVER OBJECT YOU TO DRAW AS A BOX. WHEN BOTH THE SIDES OF THE BOX ARE PARALLEL TO HORIZON LINE (I.E FLAT SID IS FACING YOU . YOUR DEALING WITH ONE POINT PERSPECTIVE. MOST OF THE COMIC STRIPES ARE BASED ON IT

THE STAR RESTING ON THE HORIZON LINE IS VANISHING POINT. TO KEEP EVERYTHING IN PERSPECTIVE, EVERY LINE TRAVELS THROUGH THE HORIZON LINE IS DISTANCE MUST CONVERGE TO VANISHING POINT

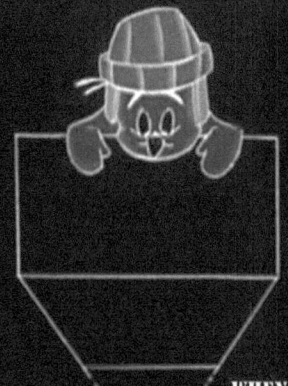

WHEN THE HORIZON LINE IS BELOW THE BOX, WE FEEL AS IF WE ARE BELOW THE BOX, LOOKING UP AT IT. WE CAN SEE THE BOTTOM OF IT

LOW ANGLE

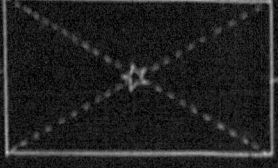

DIRECTLY ON THE HORIZON LINE

WHEN THE BOX IS CENTRED ON THE HORIZON LINE WE FEEL LIKE ITS EXACTLY AT EYE LEVEL. ONLY ONE OF THE SIDE IS VISIBLE

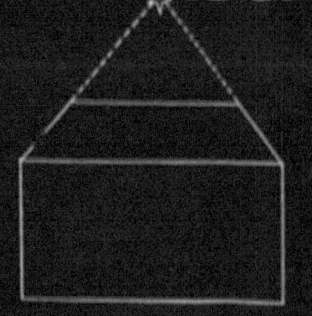

WHEN THE HORIZON LINE IS ABOVE, WE FEEL AS WE ARE ABOVE THE BOX, WE CAN SEE TOP OF IT

HIGH ANGLE

WHEN THE CORNER OF THE OBJECT IS FACES YOU, YOU CAN NO LONGER DRAW USING ONE POINT PERSPECTIVE. INSTEAD YOU SHOULD USE TWO POINT PERSPECTIVE. IN THIS DIAGRAM THE BOX IS PLACED AT ANGLE SO THE LINES ALONG THE TOP AND BOTTOM EACH SIDE, WHICH WERE HORIZONTAL IN ONE POINT PERSPECTIVE, APPEARS SLANT. SINCES THE TWO SIDE SLANT IN TWO POINT PERSPECTIVE

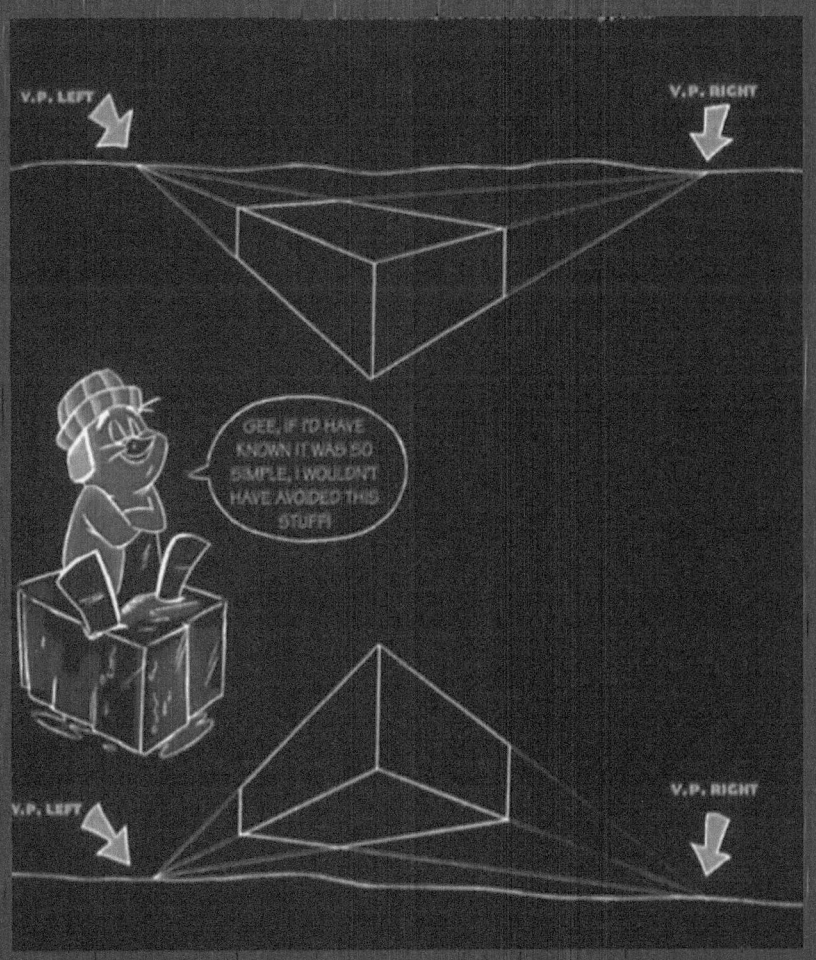

Take notes

DRAWING THE CORRECT HEIGHT OF A CHARATER IN PERSPECTIVE

HERE IS THE SIMPLIFIED WAY TO CORRTECT PROPOTION

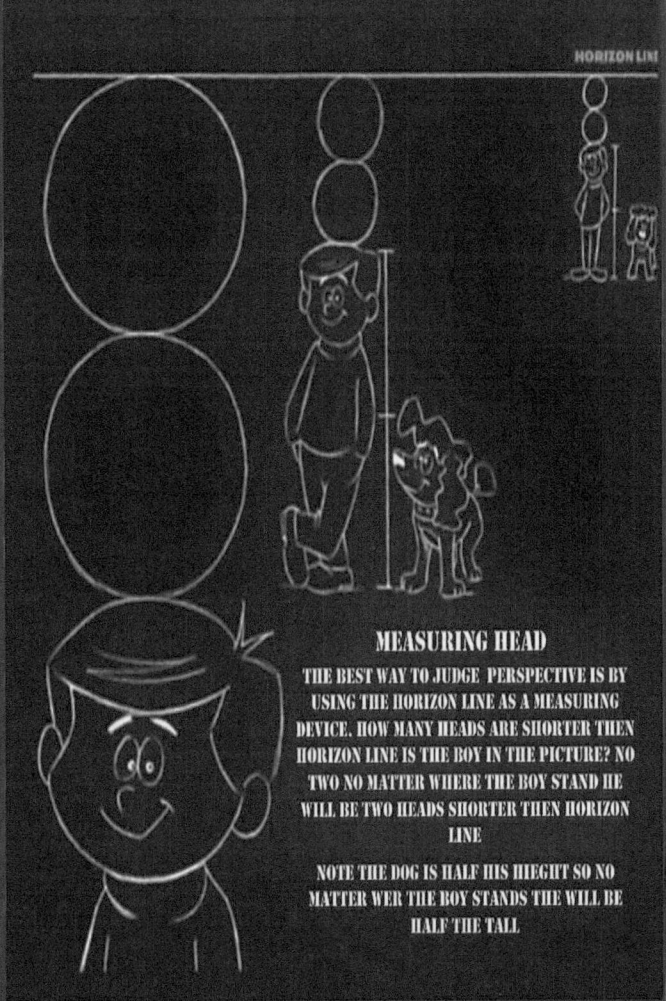

MEASURING HEAD

THE BEST WAY TO JUDGE PERSPECTIVE IS BY USING THE HORIZON LINE AS A MEASURING DEVICE. HOW MANY HEADS ARE SHORTER THEN HORIZON LINE IS THE BOY IN THE PICTURE? NO TWO NO MATTER WHERE THE BOY STAND HE WILL BE TWO HEADS SHORTER THEN HORIZON LINE

NOTE THE DOG IS HALF HIS HIEGHT SO NO MATTER WER THE BOY STANDS THE WILL BE HALF THE TALL

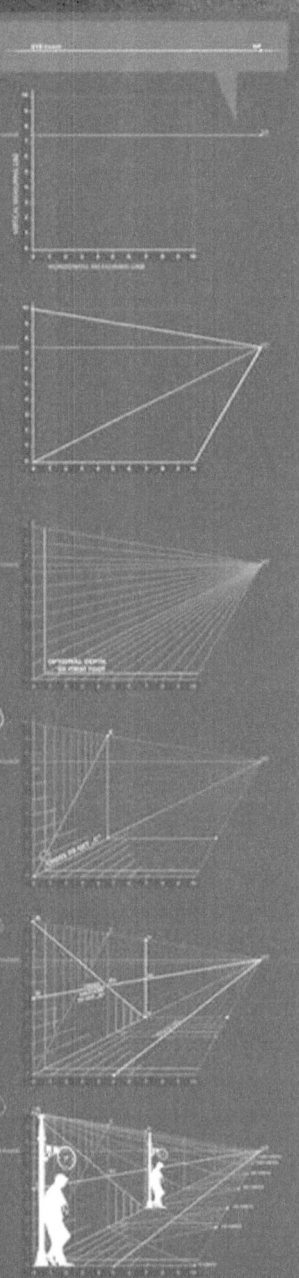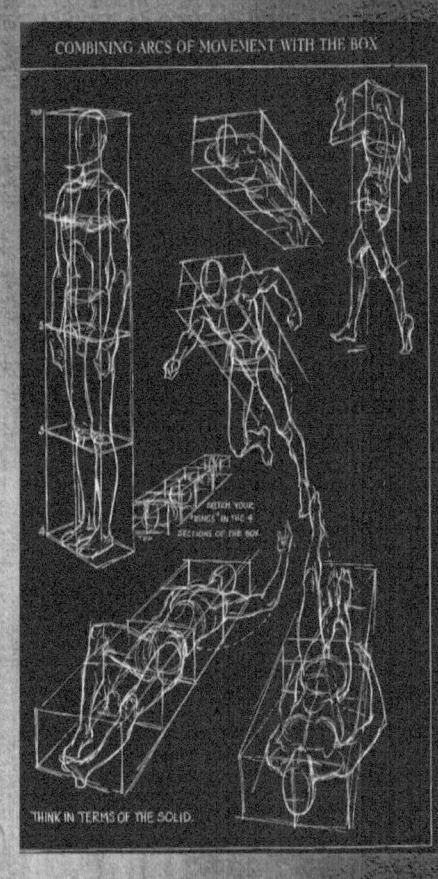

FA3

DRAWING CARTOON HOUSE USEING TWO POINT PERSPECTIVE

1. START OF BY DRAWING RECTANGLE BOX, WITH TWO VANISHING POINT

2. MARK THE TWO VANISH POINT AND ERASE ALL THE GUIDELINES

3. DRAW XS ON THE TWO SHORTER SIDES OF THE BUILDING, THE MIDDLE OF EACH X REPRESANTS THE MIDDLE SIDE OF THE HOUSE, DRAW A VERTICAL LINE THOUGH EACH ONE

4. DRAW 3 VERTICAL LINE REPRESANT TOP SIDE, FAR SIDE, NEAR SIDE OF THE ROOF. THEY SHOULD CONVERAGE AT VANISHING POINT. YOU WONT BE ABLE TO SEE THE FAR SIDE OF THE ROOF DRAW LINE ANYWAYS

TOP OF ROOF
BOTTOM OF ROOF REAR
BOTTOM OF ROOF FRONT

FA3

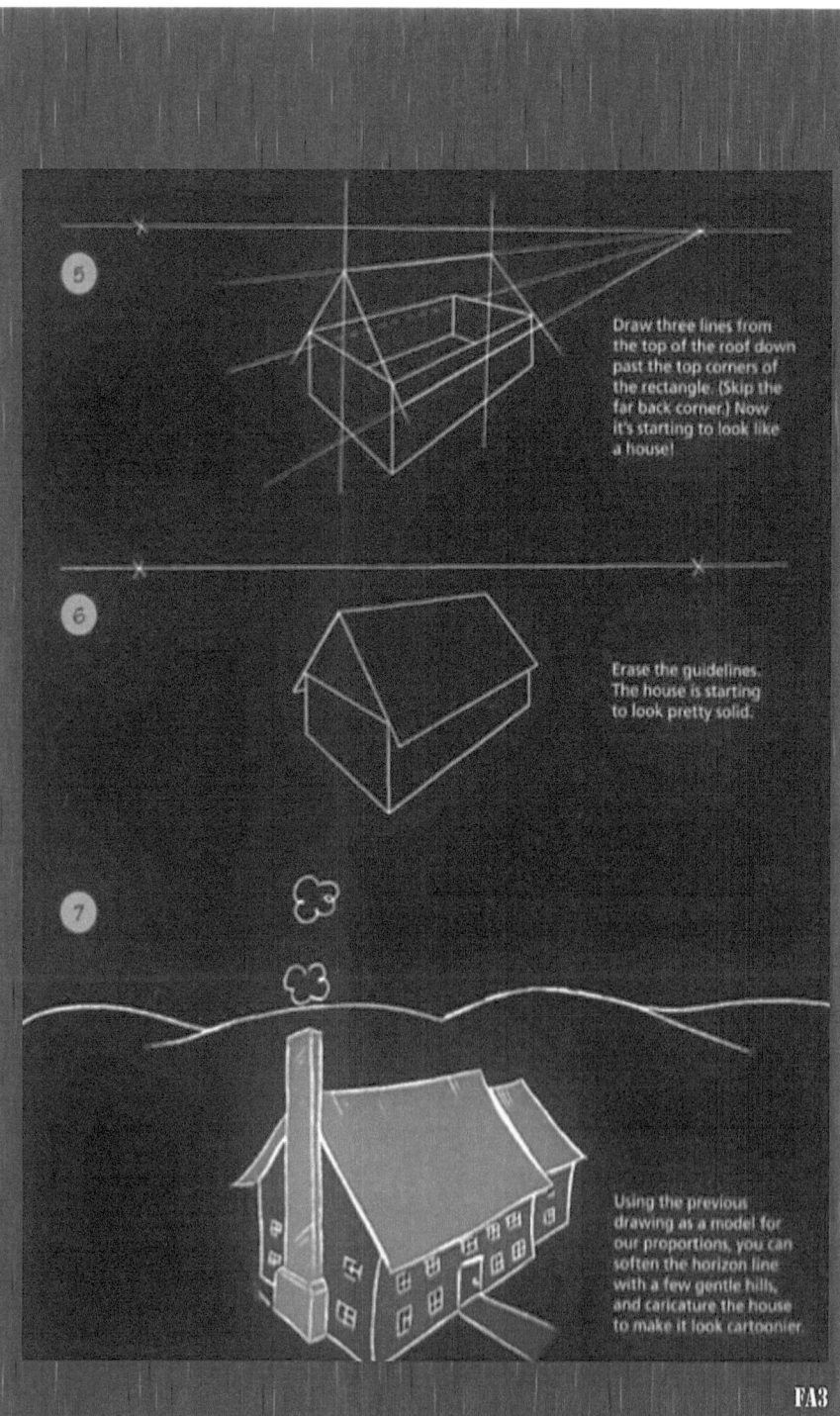

WE NEED A NICE BASE-GRID, FIRST

BUILD THE GROUND IN THE 3D-SPACE

BUILD A CUBE BASED ON THE GROUNDFLOOR

MAYBE NEED SOME LIGHT & SHADOW ?

REFLECTION AND BOUNCING LIGHT

FA3

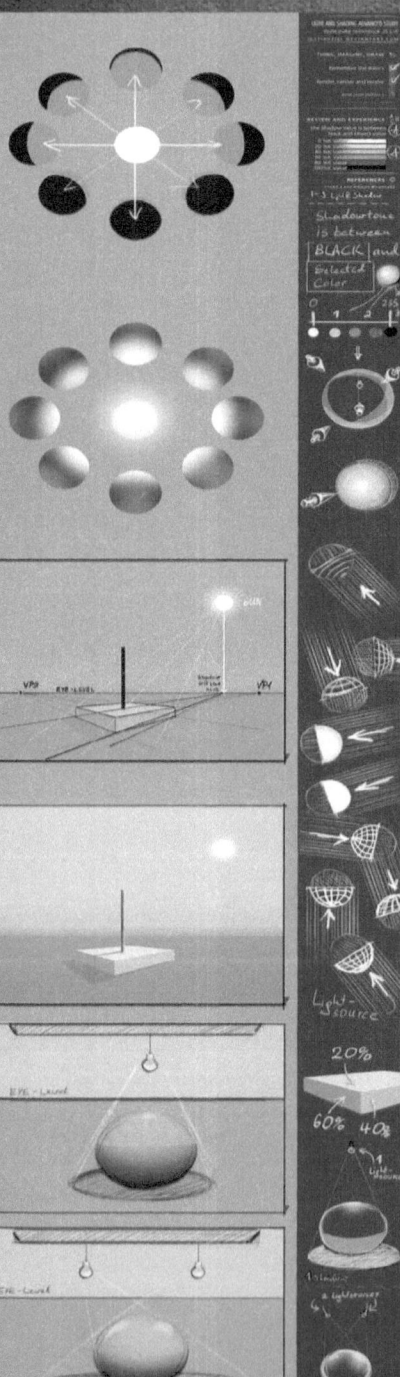

Shading techniques

FA3

Golden ratio is used by nature to create its creations, from seashell to galaxies. most famous artist like leonardo da vinci used this rule to thier art. if you want to create beautiful art use this rule no matter what kind of art from cartoons to abstract

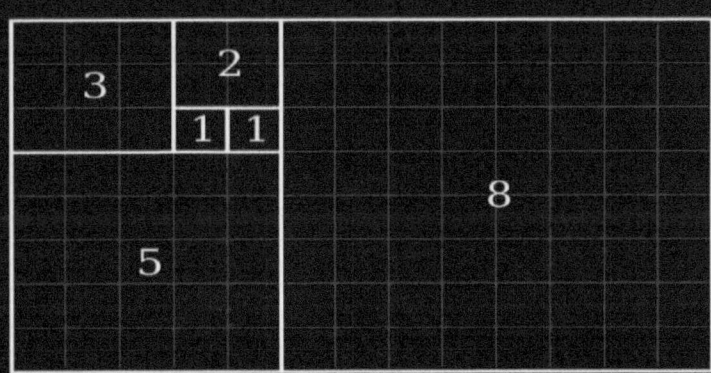
> The Golden Ratio is the relationship between two numbers on the Fibonacci Sequence...

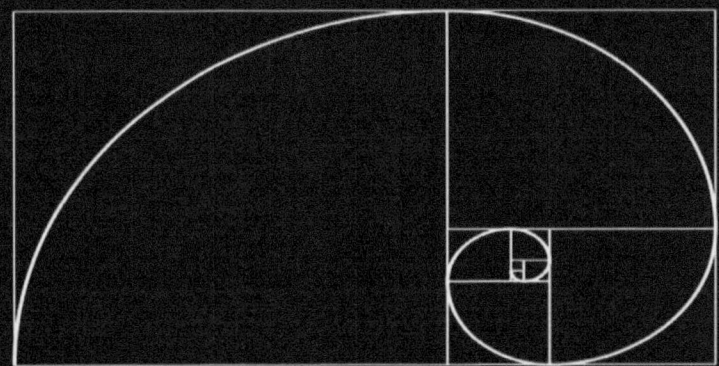
>... and plotting the relationships in scale provides us with a spiral that can be seen in nature all around us

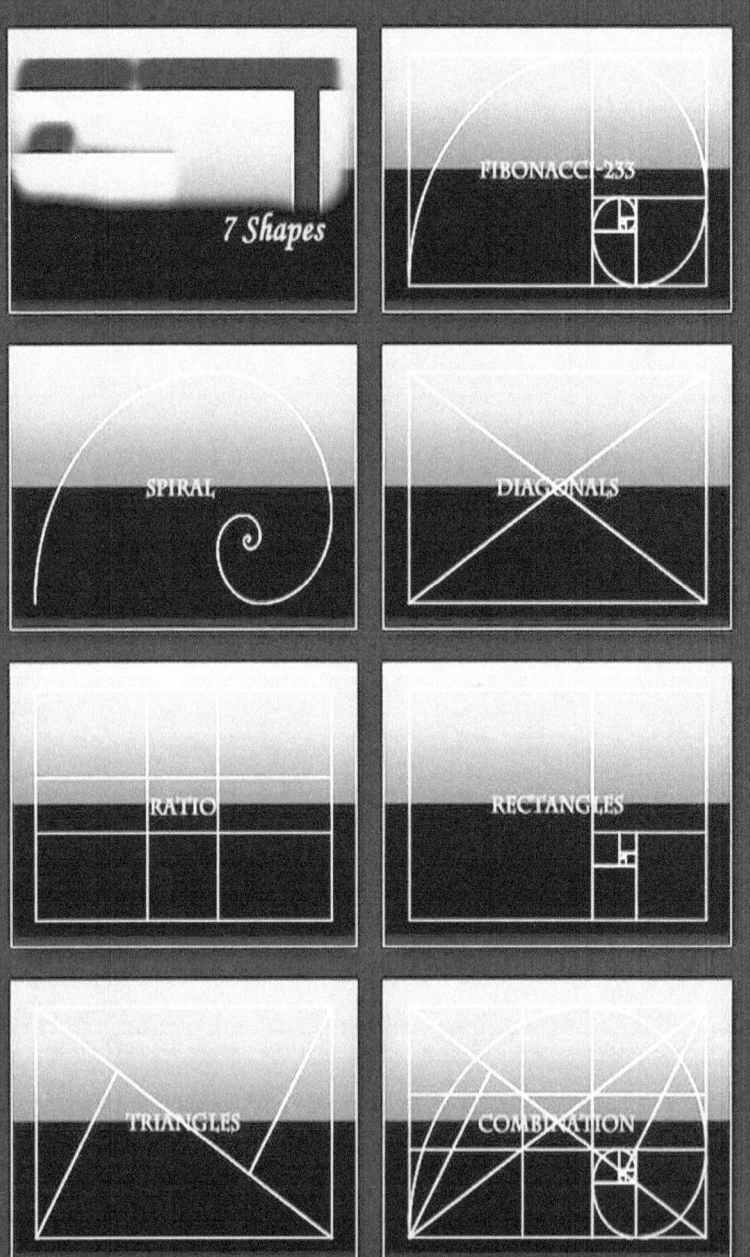

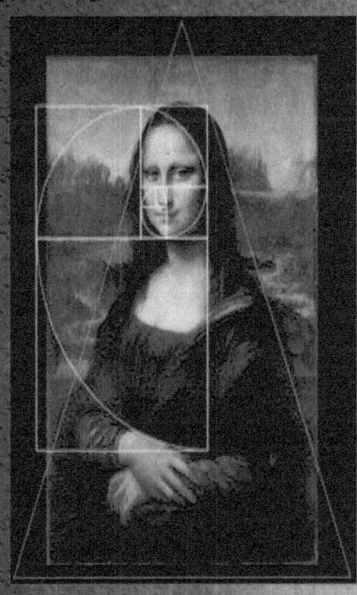
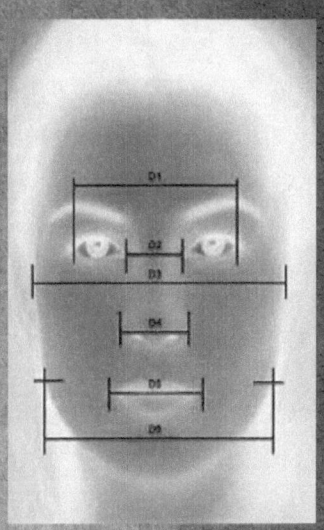
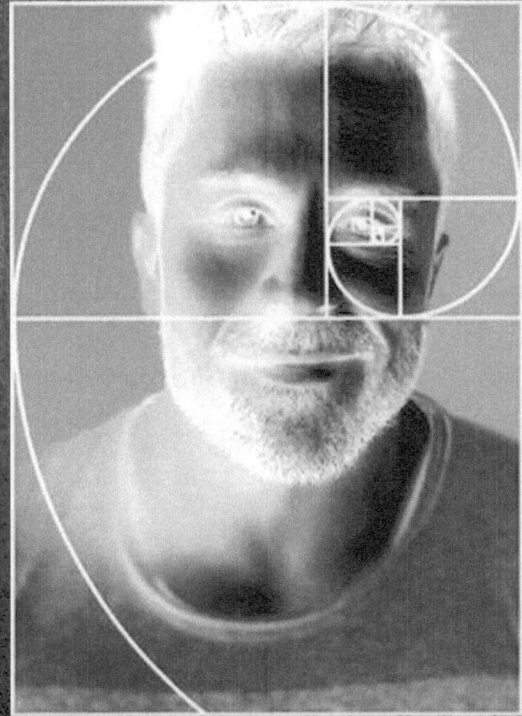

FA3

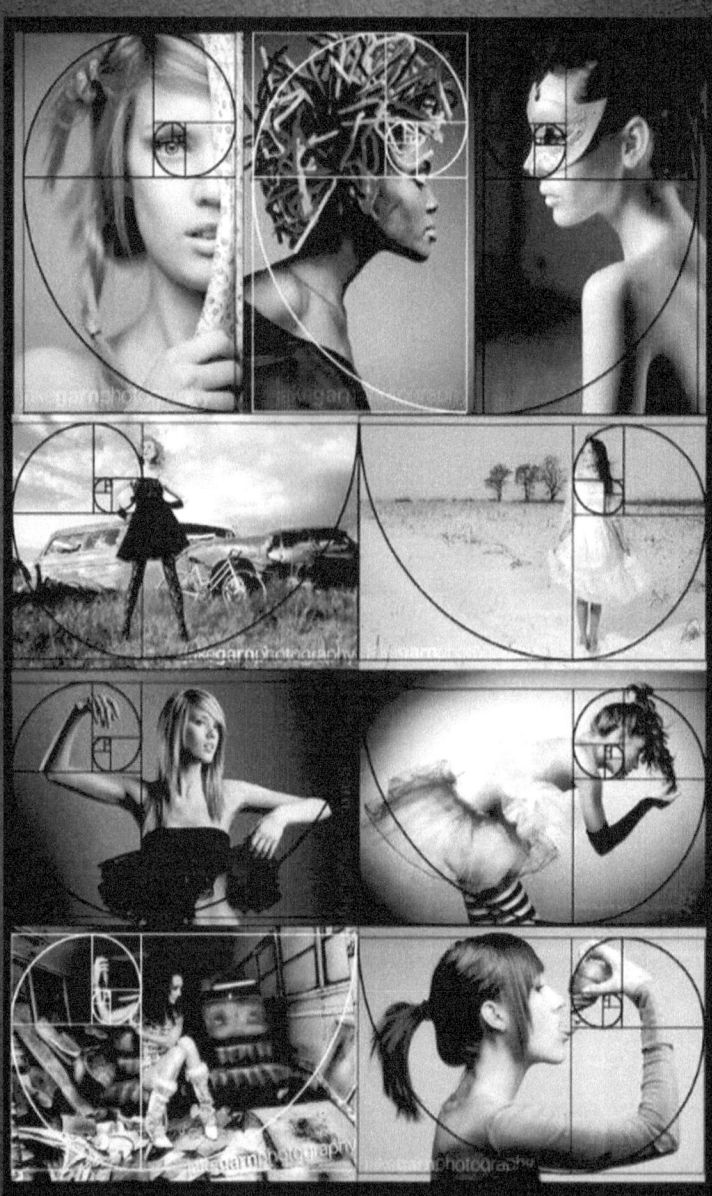

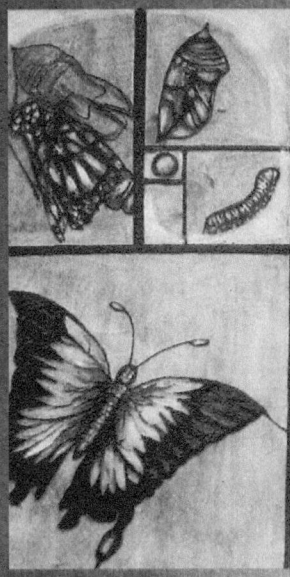
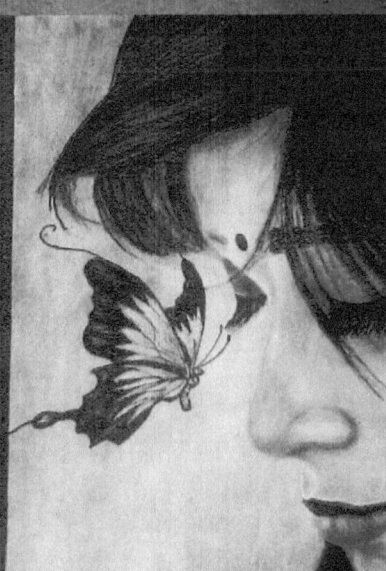
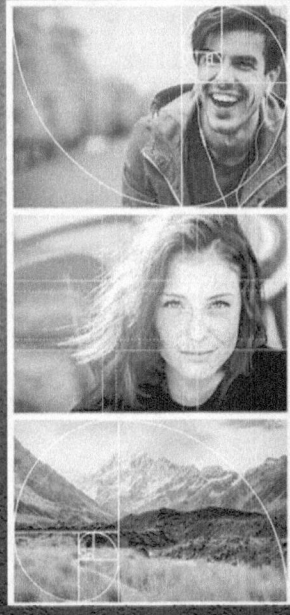

FA3

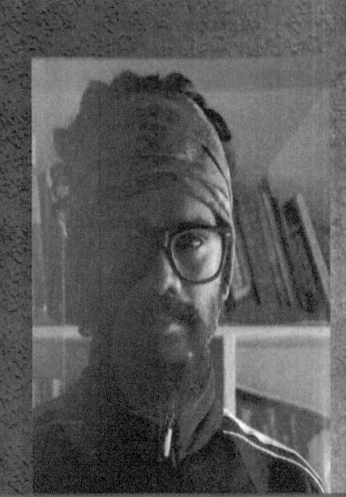

Francis Arvind. A

Art is every where but not all can understand, iam sharing the little knowledge I have in this infinity of creations

this are some basic methods if you fellow and practice till you can create your own cartoon-characters, grahic designing or any art. hope

this book will be help have fun

FA3

End of Level 1

www.ingramcontent.com/pod-product-compliance
Lightning Source LLC
Chambersburg PA
CBHW031447210526
45464CB00005B/2364